To Diane

## Stories of My Century

*Mary Mathieson*

# Stories of My Century
### a memoir by
### Mary Mathieson

"Persons attempting to find a motive in this narrative will be prosecuted; persons attempting to find a moral in it will be banished; persons attempting to find a plot in it will be shot.
BY ORDER OF THE AUTHOR
per
G. G. CHIEF OF ORDNANCE"

– Mark Twain, The Adventures of Huck Finn, 1885

© 2013 by Mary Mathieson

All rights reserved. No part of this publication may be reproduced, stored in a retrieval system, or transported in any form or by any means, electronic, mechanical, photocopying, recording, or otherwise without prior written permission of the publisher.

Library and Archives Canada Cataloguing in Publication

Mathieson, Mary, author
Stories of my century : a memoir / by Mary Mathieson.

1. Mathieson, Mary. I. Title.

ISBN 978-1-304-52734-9 (pbk.)

CT310.M394A3 2014         971.06         C2013-908406-1

In 2013, a 65 year old woman named Diana Nyad was the first person to swim the 110 miles from Havana, Cuba to Key West, Florida non-stop without the use of a shark cage. Nyad had failed three times before she finally made it. This time she came out of the water saying, "You are never too old to chase your dreams." Hearing this, I felt this woman was a kindred spirit.   - Mary Mathieson

editor: Bob MacKenzie
photo graphics: Geoff Webster

# INTRODUCTION

    I've found that remembering any particular experience has irretrievable gaps between the vivid images. This doesn't seem to spoil the overall picture.

    For instance I don't recall what mental turmoil preceded my unexpected launch into local journalism back in my Etobicoke days. I can only see myself chairing a women's church meeting at which one of my cohorts was a free-lance journalist called Virginia Etherington. I regarded her with envy knowing she even sometimes appeared in the Globe and Mail. I was determined to at least have a try at her game. Since I always preferred the pen to the tongue when dealing with a problem I found the courage to write Virginia a note asking for help. The remembered sentence from that missive was, "I have nothing to recommend me but fifty years of inexperience." (Note: that makes it 1969.)

    The immediate reply from Virginia was..."Just sit down and write about whatever appeals to you and take it into The Etobicoke Press office. They happen to be looking for a local reporter." I have no idea what inspiration resulted in my written donation but I do recall entering the unimposing office in a strip mall on Dundas Street and presenting it to an unsmiling older woman at the desk. My heart pounded as she read it through, then looked up and said, "Hmmm...you write pretty well. Come in on Monday at ten." Speechless I nodded my head and tottered out.. I didn't even ask how much my labour was worth.

    Thus began one of my happiest adventures. My column was to be called "West of Martingrove". Armed with a list of organizations and people to contact each week I gathered news of upcoming events at City Hall, The Board of Education, the YMCA , the Sea Cadets, etc. Each Monday I would sort through my gathered lore and compose that week's account on my trusty typewriter, Twinkle the cat banished from the room where he loved assisting me with the keys. I had yet to enter the computer age. This document would be delivered early Tuesday morning and the weekly rag appeared each Wednesday. It soon became clear that my copy was accepted as is. I even ventured into commentary of my own. Nobody of the small staff had time for such a nicety as editing.

I got a kick out of being included as a member of the staff on their jolly Christmas greeting card!

Only one misfire remains in my mind. I had written praising the wonderful maple syrup that was available from Quebec. An irate subscriber called the office to say it was too bad I didn't know that Ontario had every bit as good syrup as P.Q.! In haste I wrote an apology for my "sticky wicket"! Later I found that the complainant was Doug Day who forgave me and became a dear friend.

My career as a journalist came to a rather ignominious end the following June after just seven months. I happened also to be a wife and the mother of a young boy and there was no way that I could stay home from two months at the cottage just because I was playing at having a career. I had to resign. By chance (there really was no connection) the Etobicoke Press folded that summer. In recognition of his support for my effort husband Ron had collected every one of my columns and put them into a large scrapbook as a lasting memento. Coming upon it as I packed up to move some years later I realized that none of it meant anything to me let alone to posterity. It was consigned to the recycle bin with perhaps a sniffling tear or two. Requiescat in pace (or words to that effect).

The stories that follow have been incubating in my mind since the early 1990's. They began their lives as part of "Mostly From Memory…Mary's First Thirty Years". ..a launching into family Memoirs that was like turning on a tap when I sat down at my computer. A few years later the urge to add "More Memories" was just as much an outpouring. I didn't stop to plan or maintain proper chronology or follow any other rules. I was too busy including the stories of every family member past and present and every incident and event I could dredge up. Paragraphs or chapters were irrelevant. For family members the resulting bound copies were an unqualified success. Mission accomplished.

Then, as the years (what is left of 94 of them) slipped away, the desire to do a more professional job of all the stories buried in that unwieldy manuscript became a slight obsession. Editor friend Bob MacKenzie suggested I establish a Blog site to see how the new approach would work out. That proved to be just what I needed. I found out what fun it could be to give those tales full rein one at a time and get some feedback from Blog readers.

Finally the supply of material was running out . Turning the final collection into an acceptable book the next daunting step. I can't resist Bob's reaction by E-Mail to my decision to forge ahead that still makes me chuckle, "I think it's great that you believe in yourself enough to jump off the cliff without looking but cautious enough to bring along a parachute and your easy chair." An exact description of my dilemma.

So…like the New Zealander who did a "Blog to Book" and ended up #4 on the Best Seller List" in his country, what is there to lose?  At this final "INTRO" stage of MY CENTURY OF STORIES my hope is that readers will settle in their own easy chairs…enjoy reading the result… and have a few chuckles of their own.

## 1. LIFE IN THE TWENTIES

My memories first took me back into the rambling brick family home in Strathroy, Ontario...up the narrow stairway from the second floor to the dusty joists of the attic. There I could rummage among the events of the past buried in the cobwebby corners.

Hmmm. Rummaging in the attic reveals an interesting account of life in our town back in the '20's in one dusty corner. I can see myself lying on my chubby (fourish) stomach on the floor with brother Ted (three years older), the big well-thumbed British news magazines "The Sphere" and the "Illustrated News" spread out around us. We are gaping at page after page of sepia drawings of soldiers shooting their guns in battle...intrigued but not really knowing what it is all about. To us at best it is ancient history. When we were older we realized that World War 1 had ended only a scant few years before. Ted was actually born half way though it. With no radios, TV's or photos by reporters on the spot, Canadians had to wait weeks for newspapers and these artist depictions to come by boat across the ocean before they learned what had really happened on those battle fields. Even phones were new and not too satisfactory. We were fortunate not to have had a family member's name on the list of casualties in the paper.

Having none of my own I did manage to get a picture of the downtown Strathroy street lined with the early Ford cars just beginning to threaten the familiar horse-drawn wagons that had taken care of all kinds of farm work and deliveries for centuries. There is Stepler's drugstore sign as it should be and all the other local businesses lining the sidewalk and what looks like a Saturday crowd that had driven as usual in from the country after work to sample the wonders of town life. The only eatery was in the Queen's Hotel dining room...available just to the well-to-do. Tales of all night Saturday brawls proved that ale and spirits were handily available. We did know Prangley's Ice Cream Parlour that could provide a cone or soda on a summer evening and a chance to relax on their spindly parlour chairs. They also had Vanilla or Neapolitan bricks to be carted home at speed and sliced up for a cool treat as the family gathered on the veranda before the ice cream melted.

There were no freezers yet and blocks of ice were one of the deliveries for those with a kitchen ice-box. The big heavy cubes had been cut out of the local outdoor rink and packed in straw to be hefted by a muscled driver onto the wagon and later into the houses. Another "Dobbin" would pull the milk delivery wagon from the Dairy up to the back door where an aproned housewife would answer the familiar driver's knock probably welcoming a morning chat. He had a tin pint or quart pitcher to pour the day's request into her jug. Each farmer's donation to the Dairy, in big milk cans had been picked up at the end of each farm road to go into the Dairy in town. Pasteurizing came as a new wonder that kept us all safe from TB and other infections that raw milk had been found to carry. Inventions of all kinds were bringing our somewhat primitive living up-to-date. One was the milk bottles to be left at the kitchen door, replacing the tin pitchers...but with their own hazard. Leave them outside too long in the winter and they would freeze...blowing the milk out the top and breaking the bottle. A splendid sight for us kids. London's Silverwoods Dairy had their own kind with a bulbous top so that the cream (no homogenizing yet) could be ladled out first with a bent spoon. Another important "wagoneer" steered his pair up to the customer's basement window and manoeuvered his load of coal down the chute with mighty clangs into the coal bin.

Thinking of deliveries stirs memories of more irregular ones. There were occasional carts with fish packed in ice that had come in from the east coast by train. Their long journey had not improved their odor or taste and I still have nasty memories of having to eat the cooked glob. I even disliked the grubby little man who drove the wagon as though the unpleasant fish were his fault! Friday was fish day and no excuses. Then there was the tinker with the pots and pans hanging from his cart banging together and sending out a chorus of musical clatters as he drove along shouting his wares. They could be bought or he would mend your damaged one at hand. The knife grinder was always welcomed as he trundled along on foot pushing his "honing" machine. We were fascinated when the gypsies in their colorful clothing drove into town from their camp in the country in their gaudily painted wagon. We were told to give them a wide berth for fear they might kidnap us. We were scared and at the same time tempted by their exotic appearance. I doubt there was any evidence of such horrors. The Romany people have never seemed able to clear their name of that reputation.

Not surprisingly delivery wagons offered the young a fun way of getting a free ride, especially since they were forbidden both by families and the drivers. The boys mostly would run along behind until they could grab a piece of jutting wood and heave themselves aboard. Not to be outdone by their tormenters the girls tried too and mighty was the scolding I got and the howling tears I shed the day I tore my school dress and skinned my knees. Ah youth!!

Mary's favorite Treasure of the Twenties, on the old side steps in Strathroy with brother Ted.

Mary age three in Lake Huron at Grand Bend.

Dampier siblings from the top down in 1920's wardrobe. Comfort was not an option!

A younger Dapper Dad at his bank, The Bank of Commerce, circa 1900, waxed mustache and all!

The Bank of Commerce Building still in good shape in Strathroy. We called it "Dad's Bank" but it is now a thriving restaurant.

L. H. Dampier, retired banker and Strathroy Mayor, on the family's lawn, circa 1920.

Sunday at "Gastons"...Marjorie and Mary with cousin Dickie English and pug dog Pat with great Aunt Minnie and Great Aunt Cecelia in the background...circa 1924.

## 2. MORE TWENTIES - WHERE IT ALL STARTED

Sitting among the cobwebs I can spot lots more of those early experiences to browse through...even though not exactly a comfy place to sit. My lengthy life and the stories about it started in the small Western Ontario town of Strathroy. If you were to travel west out of London for a half hour or so today you would find a thriving town of 10,000 or so souls that is really a bedroom extension of the city of London. When I returned along that road after an absence of many years I was sad to find only three buildings from my past still standing to greet me. My departure was in 1932 so what could I expect?

Strathroy then was a typical Western Ontario town of tree-shaded unpaved streets lined with stately family-sized brick homes for the gentry and more modest but still brick cottages for the less affluent. Ours was quite handsome with a wrap-around veranda on a spacious corner lot just two doors from our public school on Metcalf Street and the Anglican rectory and our church around the corner on Head Street. All verty handy. There was a nice little hospital in town but babies were allowed to arrive on their own premises which I did on April 10, 1919. In actual fact Dad was serving a term as Mayor of the town at that time. I was the fourth child of his second marriage to Edith English. When I arrived mother was only 34 years old while he was 65...a disparity in age which guaranteed any children would be fatherless while they were still young. What was not evident was that they would first be motherless. In keeping with the times, the young mother had her family in rapid succession...my siblings Marjorie, Larry and Ted each just over a year apart...and then me after a three year breather for Mom. The next one was expected when I was just over two in 1921 but neither mother nor baby survived. This was not unusual, probably due to the lack of pre-natal care and good hygiene in those days. The little girl was named Edith Isabel after her mother and was buried along with her in the family plot with carved headstone in the cemetery on the outskirts of town. The very occasional times when I managed to visit, gazing at the small markers beside the big stone, I felt a nostalgic sadness for those two lives having such untimely ends. Not least of the tragedies was the mother having to leave four small, active, boisterous young children in the care of a father already retired from his position as manager of the local branch of the Bank of Commerce (not yet including the "Imperial" part). Single Dads of children so young are usually a lot younger themselves than Dad was.

Violet and Mary beside the long gone little St. Ola Station where the family arrived from Trenton in the early days.

St. John's Anglican Church, Head Street, Strathroy

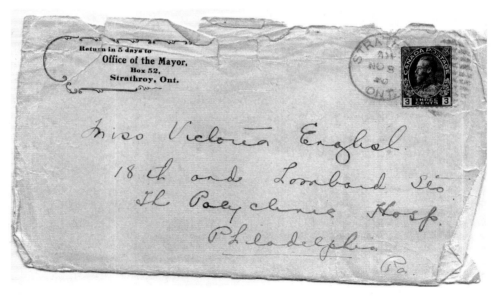

Envelope from mother's letter to her sister Victoria, bearing a 3-cent stamp, 1920.

## 3. DAD AND THE MONSTER

Remember the story when the coal had gone down the chute into our cellar? Well...one of my favorite bedtime reads is the Canadian author Robertson Davies' "Diary of Samuel Marchbanks" written in those 20's. It can still make me laugh especially when recounting Samuels's running feud with his coal furnace. Both he and Dad waged constant war on those bulky but all important monsters. We kids were wide-eyed as we lurked on the stairs at night hoping to catch some of the colourful language drifting up from the basement. We knew the routine. The trick was for Dad to stoke up the fire to last the night but not burn the house down. Then first thing in early morning down those stairs he went still in his nightshirt and once again with a lurking audience while praying volubly that the fire hadn't died in the night. If muttered imprecations came blasting up the stairs we knew he now had the daunting task of getting it "up" again. Dad was convinced that old iron monster was out to get him. On good mornings when the embers still burned and he had won, breakfast was peaceful. The bad days we kept out of sight. Keeping a supply of coal on hand meant having the delivery wagon arrive regularly. As reported the coal dust blackened delivery man would put a chute through the open basement window and pour a ton or so of the sooty chunks into our bin. Reluctant Larry and Ted grumbled at having to sift the ashes and get the pails of "clinkers" out to be picked up by the dump wagon that came by...chores often neglected, bringing father's wrath down on their unrepentant young heads. The clinkers had become hard lumps with very sharp points that made handling them a risky business. Even when the furnace performed well our house temperature hovered in the high 50's. I used to wonder why our visitors seldom took their coats off and why our current housekeeper spent so much time in her "jumbo" sweater. At one point in the mid-twenties, Dad decided to change his strategy by converting to a new-fangled oil furnace. This involved having the storage tank for the oil buried in our backyard...a fascinating entertainment for us young fry. We would hang about chewing the gummy stuff used to seal windows...ugh....until shooed away. After a trial run, father decided he didn't care for the new technology. It hadn't improved his vocabulary. He converted back, at considerable expense, to his old enemy. The storage tank is probably still there.  He did install an automatic "fireman" a new invention that helped him in the ongoing battle, even if he never won the war.

## 4. A SINGLE DAD AT 67

One story leads to another in that cobwebby attic. As recounted, poor grieving and aging Dad had joined the ranks of single fathers at the age of 67...with four little spalpeens (Irish for imps) to bring up and launch into the world. His first priority was to find a housekeeper. We had no relatives able to take on such a rugged responsibility as the care of 4 children ages 2 to 6 of which I was the youngest. The first woman Dad hired I only vaguely remember but her name was Miss Going, which turned out to be only too apt. She was an earnest rather large and awkward woman with a perpetual worried look on her solemn face and in a constant state of harassment, particularly from the boys, Lawrence and Ted. Quiet Marjorie, the eldest, and I were easier on her. I'm afraid that may have accounted for her early demise after a couple of years. She was "laid out" in the drawing room as was customary in those days, and after the funeral Dad set about finding a hopefully more lasting replacement.

The advertising must have been through the Anglican Church. However it was done the new recruit was a Mrs. Haythornthwaite (henceforth to be called Mrs. H.), a plump soul with quantities of bunched up black hair, whose name we never shortened although it came to sound more like Mizhaythunthwayd. She was the widow of a Welshman who was trained in the Church of England Church Army. He had been posted from Britain to "the colonies", which in his case was Moosonee on James Bay, Northern Ontario, and what a shock that must have been for his plump country bred wife. He had died from an accidental gun wound in 1920 and Mrs.H. was left with no home. As we learned later her husband had acted as the clergyman in the local church, mainly attended by Cree aboriginals and his wife helped with the children in the school connected with it. I never heard that it was included in those accused in recent times of abusing their young boarders. Mrs. H. was enterprising and learned to speak Cree. She told us tales of her adventures paddling the northern rivers, the monstrous moose swimming alongside the canoe...the mosquitoes and black flies...and the babies in their snug wound-up "ticanogans" carried on their mothers' backs. She was horrified that the newborns were not bathed to remove the birth material...we now know the aboriginals had it right. Also the women washed their hair in urine...they got that one wrong! The big difficulty was that Moosonee was still cut off from the south...no train service back then. Everyone and everything came in by the northern route out the St. Lawrence river, around Labrador and down Hudson's Bay to Moosonee at the bottom of James Bay (an atlas would help here). Mrs. H. told us of making a list of everything they would need for the next year to be sent out with the boat on its annual visit. She was desperate not to leave out anything important since there would be no connection for 12 months. It was real isolation since there were no phones or radio or mail delivery of any kind. The Church Army incumbent and his family had comfortable quarters but very few of their kind to socialize with.

Mrs. H had a pretty teenage daughter Daisy with light curly hair who joined her on the month long journey by ship to their distant destination in Southern Ontario. Through sometimes stormy weather they sailed north through Hudson Bay, around Labrador and calmer waters up the St. Lawrence to Montreal. There they could relax aboard a familiar train to take them the rest of their exhausting journey to be met eventually at the station in Strathroy. With them safely settled in their own quarters the single father could finally pass over the daily care of house and young and (with a huge sigh of relief) retire to his library of books and papers behind closed doors.

My memories of Mrs. H. included her ordering us story books from "Over Home" in England...her maiden name was Lily Lambert... and a periodical that had a comic strip called "Pip, Squeak and Wilfred" in it. She cooked plain heavy meals from her Brit background, topped off with leaden suet puddings, tapioca, junket or Bird's custard while the good baking got locked away in that dining room cupboard. Eggs, for baking only, came from the crock of slimy waterglass in the basement...it was yukky for small hands reaching in to get them out. In winter rubbery carrots had been buried in earth in a wooden box nearby...no fresh veggies trucked from the U.S. then  Mrs. H. huddled over the aforementioned register, mostly letting us run wild but occasionally she played "blind man's buff" with us or "pin the tail on the donkey" in the evening. One thing Mrs.H. was terrified of was losing all her thick black hair which she wore coiled in a bun. To provide for that horror her daily combings went into a china container, with a hole in the lid for that purpose, on her dresser. From there they were transferred to envelopes and stored away to make the wig she would eventually need. Ironically she died with drawers full of combing-filled envelopes and a full head of hair! Daughter Daisy, a pretty girl, used to baby-sit me by having me tag along on her trips around town scouting for a beau. She became of marriageable age while Dad was still alive and he very generously financed the wedding when, prettily gownd in blue, she married a local boy, Frank Bartholomew, who worked at Downham's. the local Nursery. The couple was transferred to the branch in Bowmanville and I remember driving down there with them in their Model T Ford for a visit soon after. I didn't know why Daisy didn't seem very well at the time, but it was soon evident when the first of several little Bartholomews arrived on the scene. Daisy soon changed from the pretty slim bride I remember, to a blousy housewife and I understand she and Frank took mother for all they were worth over the years.

Strathroy, Ontario.
April 9th, 1907.

The Lady Superintendent,
   Evanston Hospital
      Training School for Nurses.
         Evanston, Ill.

Dear Madam :-

    I take very great pleasure in stating that I am intimately acquainted with Miss Edith I. English, who is a candidate for admission into The Evanston Hospital Training School for Nurses, having known her from childhood up. I can only say that she is one of the brightest and best of girls, and that I am satisfied she will be found to be clever and undoubtedly reliable in every respect.

    It is hardly necessary for me to add that her family and connections stand amongst the highest in this community.

Yours faithfully

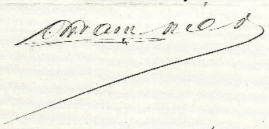

Dad's recommendation to the Evanston Hospital of his young friend Edith English, who would become his wife.

Edith English (mother) in the middle at Evanston Hospital circa 1908.

**WIFE OF EX-MAYOR IS DEAD AT STRATHROY**

STRATHROY, August 16.—Mrs. Lawrence Dampier, wife of Ex-Mayor Dampier, Metcalfe street, died suddenly to-day. The deceased was 36 years of age and the daughter of the late Mr. and Mrs. J. English. Besides her husband she is survived by two sons, Lawrence and Edward, and two daughters, Marjorie and Mary. The funeral will be held Thursday afternoon from the residence to St. John's Anglican church and interment will take place at Strathroy Cemetery.

Notice in the Strathroy newspaper on the occasion of my mother's death.

### 5. A TEENAGE ADVENTURE

I think it is safe to say that none of us ever forget that exciting day when we set out on our very first teenage adventure absolutely on our own.  My cousin Dickie and Aunt Olive were just two of the shadowy grown-ups of the English family back when, after Sunday School we kids all went on our (pretty dull) Sunday afternoon visits with Dad to our only relatives.   Growing up as we did in the depressed twenties and thirties on a severely restricted income there were very few treats.  Later in the mid-thirties with Dad now gone I was in high school and boarding in London with the rector's widow, the redoubtable Mrs. Pugsley.  None of us minded having to wear mended stockings, hand-me-downs and resoled shoes.  We were all in the same boat.  Saturday movies at 15 cents and the radio at home were our entertainment.  For me and my girl friends figuring out which of our favorite songs would be on the weekly radio Hit Parade was a major event.   Dickie and Aunt Olive were by this time well established in an apartment in Chicago.  I was ecstatic the day they invited me, age 16, to visit them by train for ten days over the Christmas holidays.  I was stunned when the all powerful Official Guardian okayed  $25.00 for the expenses.  That covered the train rides and meals and any other needs for the whole trip.  I can close my eyes even now and imagine every one of those adventurous days.  Here are some of the highlights.

...The train ride was my very first with my own plushy seat in the passenger car as it rattled along while I watched the scenery go by from my sooty window.  I can still feel the thrill of sitting proudly with other more elegant travelers at a linen, silver and crystal set table in the glamorous dining car being served food I hardly recognized by white clad waiters swaying with the rhythm of the train.   It was even more thrilling than I had imagined from those flashing glimpses when Dad had taken us to see the daily train whiz by in Strathroy.  I never dreamed that I might one day be on the inside looking out!

...Dickie and Aunt Olive had a small apartment along with their cat Sammy on the top sixth floor of what to me was a high rise.  Aunt Olive  provided  relaxing meals  and made me  feel really grown up.  We were invited for Christmas dinner at the very posh home of their friends the  Kilbournes.   It was  the first time  I had  ever had  a real cocktail  in a crystal glass  and it reduced everything  to a happy haze.  Mrs. Pugsley would not have approved. I didn't even mind eating COOKED grapefruit in a salad. I was ready for anything!

...The evening we all spent at a performance of the Ballet Russe de Monte Carlo turned me into a lifelong balletomane. My eyes were glued to the stage in our front and centre seats from start to finish while those fairylike forms in filmy tutus, gracefully floated through the air...ballet shoes "en pointe". Even the names of the three performances "Petrouchka", "La Boutique Fantastique" and "Les Sylphides" have never been forgotten. The evening went by like a flash. Of course like most girls I daydreamed of becoming one of them but like most it came to nothing. We also saw two engrossing stage plays, one called "First Lady" as I recall, and another starring a well known then but long forgotten actress, Charlotte Greenwood.

...Most exciting was that I was given bus tickets and allowed to roam the city on my own during the day when my hostesses were busy. Yes, that's Chicago I'm talking about. A good thing Aunt Olive's directions were so accurate that they kept me from getting lost since there were no cell phones to put me in touch. The streets were busy with honking cars and double decker buses but I felt relaxed and grown up and drank it all in. I remember seeing Colleen Moore's famous doll house full of beautifully crafted miniatures in rooms that were tiny replicas of splendid mansions. I have always loved any example of those small incredible works of art. The Lincoln Planetarium let me lie back and enjoy the night sky full of stars and listen to the program while the sun was shining outside.

...A particular treat for an early days radio play buff was watching one being produced live. Nothing was taped then. I loved the swaying ride atop the double decker bus when we set off to meet a cousin, Edwin Marshall, who was the director of a radio play being produced live. He let Aunt Olive and me in to watch although the public wasn't admitted as a rule...we were sworn to silence. My chief memory is of the strange mixture of wooden and metal odds and ends and liquids and other unlikely gimmicks used for sound effects, usually nothing to do with the real thing. The actors and actresses in plain work clothes read their scripts into mikes but they had to use artistry to make the play come alive for an unseen and unseeing audience. I was entranced. I've always preferred radio plays where I could close my eyes and use my imagination to provide the pictures instead of watching someone else's version on a TV screen.

That is a treasure still clearly remembered.

Bathing beauties at Bruce Beach, 1937.

Portable Victrola at Bruce Beach 1937.

Sleepy beauties Ruth, Miriam, Max, Barb, and Elizabeth. Kay and Mary up front, Bruce Beach, 1937.

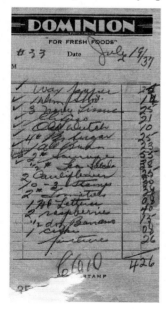

Grocery bill: Bruce Beach. Cost of living, 1937.

### 6. MARON MANOR

After Ron and I decided to marry in the Spring of 1951 we were faced with finding a house to settle into. (I had a private prayer that we could avoid sharing digs with my in-laws nice though they might be) There were some roadblocks. Happy to be out of the Air Force and being an unattached bachelor, Ron had happily spent his demob bonus on enjoying a spendthrift holiday at Banff. He had a job at Ontario Hydro but that was it. With no family backing I sported the same zero bank balance. In the few years of peace since 1945 very few strides had been made in house building. In the whole of Toronto there was one middle class subdivision in the making in the east end and one in the west. Fortunately Ron had a friend with some influence in the Saracini development at Martingrove and Burnhamthorpe in the west end. By some trickery they overcame our lack of a minimum income and allowed us to put $1000 down on a $10,000 storey-and-a-half with a $9000 20-year mortgage at 4%. My upcoming mother-in-law Dr. Lily B. Mathieson was the heroine of this transaction in lending us that down-payment. How Ron managed it is a mystery since he repaid her in one year! With the deal closed I was ecstatic and came up with that name in the title...Maron Manor...that used both ours. Ron was so sure we were on our way to bankrupcy that he had no heart for clever names and it never took off except with me.

I will tease you with an event that will come up in a later chapter. While we were looking over the several models on the property, Ron had brought along a more experienced Hydro friend for support. I was amused to see him pacing around and muttering as he examined every aspect of the lots which seemed quite unnecessary. Finally he gave his blessing to one particular one which we forthwith accepted as our choice.

By the way...this future domicile was on a clay-mud lot with an unpaved driveway and no culvert Grass was a dream away. Inside boasted a base coat of paint on the woodwork only...not the walls, floors unfinished, no fixtures. Facing a mammoth list of necessary To Dos simply could not dampen our joy at having a place of our own. Note: We were at the western edge of Etobicoke with signs of more building underway but mostly farmers' fields and markets stretching west. Mississauga did I hear you say? Not even a whisper of it, or of Hazel McCallion, on the horizon!!!

Fast forward to moving in day after the May 5 nuptials and trip to New York (Hey...another fun story there!). Having run out of cash we had spent the final night at sister Violet's house. I was one big toothy smile as we rolled into the lumpy driveway at 5 Northglen Ave. and staked our claim. That I believe was a Sunday and I soon noted a guilty look on the Master of the Manor's face. It turned out to be because he had invited all his friends (at least fifteen) to come for a housewarming the coming Thursday on Arbor Day. Just forgot to tell me! He hadn't even made it a pot luck…just suggested they bring something to plant since that apparently was the point. Aw come on Ron…in clay mud????

My brief memories of that event include making potato salad in a preserving kettle!. The rest of the food is a blur. I noted someone wandering around with an armful of lilacs. The next sighting was of them neatly arranged in the bathroom receptacle. Don't know how the guests got round that one but one of the pre-school tads simply christened our front hall. Planting? Yes some brave souls hacked away with picks and shovels with sweat pouring and managed to deposit their donations. One shrub actually survived.

That was the first of many happy gatherings. Obviously I've deserted the attic and am using the chair with pictures and all the furnishings, each with a history, to jog my memory.

Bridesmaid Marjorie and bride Mary Dampier, with the Blackburn children Martha, Walter Jr. and Susan, May 5, 1951.

Wedding pictures: Mary and Ron
May 5. 1951.

## 7. BARE BUILDINGS BLOG–MUSINGS

This relaxing time I have another unlikely topic that intrigues me. I know…"Buildings I have Known" sounds really dullsville but bear with me. When you think about it we deal with multi kinds of them. We've lived, gone to school, worked and even played in them. I've never really taken to the idea that inanimate objects have a life of their own. Older cultures did and even worshiped them. Just the same I have been nudged by bricks and mortar personalities more than once A sharp eye and ear gives them away and even the people who belong in them.

A leisurely drive down a residential street for instance. That house on the corner is set in beautifully landscaped and manicured lawns and gardens. A weed would think twice before rearing its ugly head. The windows in the handsome house shine with elegance and the paint is impeccable. Isn't that a sculptured concrete nose above the front door…turned up at me? The residents make me feel uncomfortable without even meeting them. On the other hand another lot further down leans a little too much in the other direction. It ignores the weeds and there are signs of unwanted debris leering at me from the back yard. I wouldn't venture there for fear of meeting the dubious owner. Next in line is a comfortable rather shabby but well-tended and attractive rambling house and garden. It would be fun I think to sit in that beckoning chair in the shade with a cool drink and chat with the pleasant lady doubtless living inside. Anyway…there's nobody to prove me wrong!

Commercial buildings are the real conundrums. The kind of architect who designed them in the first place is obvious…but long gone. Their present personalities are riddles to be solved.. My example is a six-storey condo building in a pleasant suburban area. It is not crammed in among other high rises and so has open vistas for the dwellers to look out on…an important bonus. Inside, the lobby and halls are pleasant enough, clean and functional but nothing to catch the eye, and the apartments present standard layouts. To anyone considering a move it seems like a very acceptable environment. Why then when I came in was one of those upper balconies frowning fiercely at me?

That should have warned me. For instance there was a common room for use of the residents on the main floor. Inquiring about it would have revealed that it is kept firmly locked, lacking anyone who is willing to be responsible for a communal coffee hour or a friendly game of cards. The outdoor pool had a couple of chairs but no umbrellaed tables to escape the sun and no shade trees near or welcoming play paraphernalia. These drawbacks remained unnoticed so I did move in and I did stay for a little over a year but as a single senior with no wheels I made haste to move out before another winter imprisoned me. I came to nod and say a few words to neighbors in the hall but sociability ended there. When I left I said goodbye to the friendly caretaker and nobody else. That balcony that had glowered at me on my way in was still doing so as I exited for the last time. Maybe it would have a smile for an upwardly mobile couple with wheels. Nevertheless...Caveat emptor ...buyer beware.

## 8. A NON-FAN'S MEMORIES OF GREY CUP

It was that picture of the early versions along the side of the front page of the November 24$^{th}$ (2012) Saturday Star that did it. But come on guys...I don't go back that far! In fact football was never my sport of choice...it just kept turning up on my agenda uninvited. Living in London the Western Mustangs were our football heroes and our high school crowd back in the thirties was encouraged to support them by getting game tickets for 25 cents. Pretty reasonable I agree but we didn't have all that many quarters to spare. My one venture into the Western open air stadium was a disaster never repeated since nobody had told me to dress super warmly and I shivered and froze all afternoon. Later as a Western student I had no choice and rah-rahed with the best of them at every home game, wearing the required big yellow mum. I really enjoyed the half time show more than the play, led by a high stepping majorette with band leader Don Wright, later of music fame, inspiring the Western band to perform while we cheered and clapped.
And to think that my dear friend Morley Thomas was on the team, tearing up and down the field. He was still unknown to me. Morley is now the only remaining Mustang of his vintage and was honored for the same this very year at a Western game. I'm still your fan Morley!!!

    Oh yes...the Grey Cup. Fast forward to the Fifties and husband Ron and his crew of Hydro buddies who were diehard Argo fans. Every year on the day of the game we gathered at the perennial host's house loaded with chips and dips and...yes bottles. In the oven were racks of spareribs simmering gently as we noisily followed the play all afternoon on the newly acquired TV. Like the time the fog was so dense we couldn't even see the players. They had to try again the next day I think? The party was the standard Grey Cup orgy which we became less and less enthusiastic about as the years passed. The exciting times were when the game was being played right in Toronto with the hordes of westerners in cowboy mode and Stetson hats descending whooping from the trains several days ahead of time and never stopped cooking up pancakes and stomping and whooping for the duration. Still happening?
I'm safely out of it. We always went to the big parade and a memory there is of being packed into a crowd on Yonge Street, waving at some of our party on the other side and unable to cross over to join them. As for the Royal York...all the furniture and valuable artifacts were always stowed away from the huge lobby. It was impossible to cross over there either and great fun to welcome the prancing horse that was the star

attraction. The police stood well back from the mayhem with their fingers crossed.

One year the Winnipeg Blue Bombers were playing in Toronto. Ron's cousin was a doctor in Winnipeg and a mad fan of the team. She had planned to come and the fact that she broke her leg just before the trip was not about to stop her. She flew in and arrived at the parade, leg encased in a caste, escorted in style with wheelchair and crutches. She was the one we couldn't cross Yonge Street to reach. Did Winnipeg crown her trip with victory??? I could make it up but I just don't remember. She survived to walk again on both legs though.

Yes…I keep watching, at least partly…in honour of those happy days of yore!

A receipt from the Royal York, October 31, 1937.

## 9. CHRISTMAS BACK THEN

My stories have suffered from a bad dose of neglect. Among other things the whole long Christmas Season of 2012 played interference. Climbing up the attic stairs now that it is over and rummaging around for signs of Christmas in the 20's makes a good way to get back on track.

Here goes. For us young tads this was the most important event of the year. Because we lived in frugal times, the turkey-and-presents side of Christmas had far more importance even than it does now. As kids we had very few "boughten" toys and no new ones except at Birthdays and Santa Claus time. The ones we had were cherished...often hand-me-downs like our clothes. My brothers' ancient train had scarred heavy metal coaches, hard to push around as they had to be by hand but precious just the same. We managed a ball for catch, mostly for the boys who kept girls out of anything they could, and a skipping rope for the girls. The wagon was a family affair and we managed "bob skates"...two runners attached to our shoes for the outdoor rink...the same one where the ice blocks for home delivery were made. The Christmas season didn't begin until a week or so ahead and there were no colored lights or Christmas music blaring away either inside or out to remind us of the festivities to come...just piles of seasonal snow. Just the same there was a build-up of excitement once December came and the school holiday loomed. One gift to and from each family member was the limit so our secret list was short requiring much pencil chewing. A letter to Santa would be sent off to the North Pole but the Post Office ignored them and we never expected an answer. Even when we got our first battery radio there was no fanfare as Santa's sleigh flew across the sky pulled by his reindeer...and Rudolph with a red nose wasn't born yet! Of course there was the Sunday School concert we hated to be lived through, organized by prim white-haired no-nonsense Miss Stephenson. I never forgot the year I only made it as the ugly sister...my pretty blond classmate won the Cinderella role I coveted. The performance always ended with a "Noel" solo by an aging chorister and rousing carol singing by the whole congregation.

Shopping and making the pudding were in the last few days and we loved using the big wooden spoon and even our scrubbed hands in the gooey pudding mix.  My first year (six-years old I think) actually to go shopping was a double lesson by Dad.  I was round-eyed as he showed me how he could write a cheque for one dollar and then take me to the bank to turn it into real money.   I had never felt so important.  Then on my own, clutching my wealth, off I went to the five-and-dime store to buy four presents…quite a stretch to say the least.  Small cotton hankies in a box were the best bet.   For Dad I settled on a bit of embroidery I started and promised to finish after Christmas…but never did.  The little circle of wood holding the cloth hung around for years.

      The tree went up Christmas Eve in a bucket of coal.  Ours was a cedar one reaching to the dining room ceiling and decorated Christmas Eve with red and green rope and ornaments saved over the years…no dangerous candles.   It was magic even if the limbs drooped and were hard to hang anything on. We always had at least one cat so nothing hanging low.  The ceilings were festooned with more ropes and those expandable paper bells stored from year to year.  Christmas morning began with the stockings hung at the end of our beds…the long woolen ones.  I was sure I wouldn't sleep a wink Christmas Eve.  I'd be sure to hear Santa's sleigh and the reindeer arrive with his bag on the roof.  We had a nice big fireplace ready for him to come down and cookies and milk left handy.  Sadly the next thing I knew it was morning but we could dig into the stockings as soon as we woke up and find the orange and candies that had mysteriously found their way into the bulging feet. We would have skipped breakfast and headed for the presents but no dice.  Dad wasn't above tormenting us by having an extra cup of coffee to prolong the torture. Finally he led the parade to open the double drawing room doors and the rush to find which chair our pile was on. We could count on lots of mysterious white (no colored or fancy paper) tissue wrapped parcels for each of us even though the individual value was small. Quantity ruled over quality and we squabbled over them greedily.  One sad memory is of the year I had misbehaved to the extent that Dad said there had been a big parcel for me which Santa had withdrawn. The thought of that missing package almost spoiled my Christmas. Christmas morning church was at 11 o'clock and there was no possibility of missing it.  Out of our pyjamas and into Sunday best. Leaving our newfound treasures was torture. The rector didn't allow each child to bring one gift to ease the pain until years later.  The true Spirit of the Birth of the Christ Child was buried under a pile of Christmas wrappings back home.    Christmas dinner was either the traditional turkey or occasionally a goose and Dad had his hands full satisfying his young, all of whom wanted the drumstick.  Mr. Meakison, the town grocer, always gave his good customers a 5-pound box of (dubious) chocolates at the Season, and for once we were allowed to stuff ourselves to the limit...and beyond. Sick tummies were worth the price.

    I have no memory of Boxing Day sales. For us young it was the day we wrote our Thank You notes to aunts and cousins, chewing the pencils and suffering over each word before we could escape to play. These simply listed everything we had received with a thanks for the particular gift. The tradition of handwritten Thank You notes has not survived into this gift-packed century. In fact hand written anything! After that chore we were finally released to play inside or out and enjoy our stash of new things in our hard won school holidays.

    For comparison we all have a load of mental pictures of the excess we have just experienced. Spreading charity gift certificates could only ease my conscience a meager amount. And yet there are hundreds of generous souls out there who spent their time and resources to bring the happiness of the Season to all those in need. Lets all raise a post 2012 Christmas nog in their honour.

Dead of winter in far north Abitibi Canyon, only the staff house and recreation hall showing with two stalwarts. Well below zero C., 1942.

## 10. BASS LAKE AND THE CABIN

Becoming involved with Ron Mathieson in 1947 led inevitably to a close relationship with his summer passion…the family cottage. I learned that as a baby he was put down for his nap in a little hammock between two trees and (I swear) roots made their way down. Or maybe it was just in the family genes since his mother and sister shared cottage fever. Here is some "get in the mood" background. Hunter's Point reached out into a beautiful little lake about 2 ½ miles in from highway 62 that leads north from Belleville. The turn is halfway between Madoc and Bancroft. It was Ron's dentist father Dr. Will, an avid angler, who was "hooked" by some fishing buddies and in 1914 bought the small clapboard building perched on the point that served as a cottage. It was all of ten dollars. Just getting the family there was a pioneer trek. Besides the parents there was Gramma Boyington, a tiny strong feisty woman, one demure pre-teen (Violet), and one frisky one (Mary). No Ronald until 1917. They would all pile into an early morning train at the Danforth Station in East End Toronto headed for Trenton where a picnic lunch on a grassy hill filled the time. and them, as they waited for the local train to chug northward to tiny St. Ola. There a village man helped load all their food and equipment for the summer which had been sent on ahead into his horse-drawn wagon and rattled off down the road to the end of the lake. Then yet more lifting and shifting to reload into a boat whose always grumpy owner would take them the final couple of miles to the Point. Hopefully prayers had held off the rain. A downpour would be disastrous for putting up the big tent that had to be raised (dry) first thing for extra sleeping quarters. Hearing tales of those trips over the years I found it hard to believe how it was worth it. During the summer there was a small general store out by the St. Ola Station and a pastime for the young was to walk out on train day the 2 ½ miles and get the bread and few items that were available…a 5-mile round trip with side tours to check on turtles and other wild life, that happily filled the time. Of course there was swimming and canoeing in the mostly calm lake. Gramma always brought sealers of cooked meat and fishing was not just a sport. Rowing down the lake to where the blocks of ice were buried in straw and had to be hoisted into the boat was heavy and awkward…not a popular chore. Berry picking involving everyone with pails flopping around their waists meant trying to be the first to get to the fields with the best crops, ahead of other cottage pickers. The ladies entertainment meant dressing in long cotton gowns to walk through the woods and share tea with a neighbour. One enterprising woman even corralled the children for Sunday School each week. Apparently the summers were over all too soon.

    As the years passed cars and a lake road eased the trip. By my time in 1947 there were improvements to the accommodation too but the city girl was more aware of the comforts that were lacking. Still…it was a beautiful place to swim and relax. Every summer weekend Ron and I and "Sherby" the resident cat set off in the packed car on the nearly 5-hour drive. We had no pet carrier so put up with insulted meowing which often ended in a fur neckpiece for me. I counted 21 stoplights on our trip through the city. Highway 401 was beginning to appear at intervals along the way but mostly the old two-lane #2 meandered through one town after another until at Belleville the real country road headed north and wove back and forth through the woods to our destination. Not even a path to our door which meant trekking the supplies through the trees infested with welcoming mosquitoes. Sherby just took off to recover before hunger drove him home. It was several years before the road was extended to reach us and carriers were invented for puss.

    The little family cottage was still perched on the point with it's beautiful view in all directions. A boathouse that never saw a boat except as winter storage was added facing into the bay and provided pleasant additional quarters. There were always lots of visiting bodies. In 1932, 15 year-old Ron had an unexpected chance to fulfill one of his dreams. Old Mr. Wood on one of the islands had taken a fancy to Ron and when he died that year he left $100 (maybe $1500 in today's currency?) to him in his will. Ron was of course ecstatic. He also just happened to go to Murphy's Corners a few miles further along Hastings Road and see a "For Sale" sign on an old log house. In no time $10 had changed hands and local friend Bruce had been persuaded to help take it down and transport what logs could be salvaged to the site Ron had already chosen (to the family's surprise) on the crest of the hill at the edge of the Mathieson property with a splendid westward view over the sparkling lake. Those 12" logs were a hundred years old, hand-hewn and hand sawn with not a nail used. They had a soft patina somewhat enhanced in spots by long ago faded whitewash. Ron carefully had the logs numbered before loading them on Bruce's wagon. Of course the numbers disappeared in the first rainstorm. Also by the time the logs had been turned into a 28' by 18' single room the rest of his inheritance had melted away.

For the rest of the thirties Ron saved every penny from odd jobs and gifts determined to make his castle at least weatherproof...a roof with cedar shake shingles, front and back doors and windows in the roof peaks and each side of the front door cut out and a sub flooring installed. Fortunately there was no need for a moat. By the end of the decade Hitler put a stop to normal living for one and all. The cabin became a handy catchall for all kinds of boxes and tools and even an old boat. With it all pushed aside there was room for fun gatherings with dancing to recorded music and games of charades. Come demob time for Ron in 1945 the dream plans came out again and bit by bit the chinking, fireplace, proper windows and a handsome mantle donated by a cousin made the home begin to take shape. A proper flooring was laid by the laird himself but before that could happen a concerted effort involving willing and unwilling hands had to get rid of the above list of junk. A weekend of three Hydro buddies got the wiring done even if the fuse box was upside down...where it remained.

The defining moment came after the 1951 wedding. We were assigned the boathouse, pleasant enough but still under the eagle eye of Dr. Lily. We wanted out own place and I remember the day the beds were hauled up the hill under her disapproving eye. Now of course other problems popped up. To get our own meals we needed a refrigerator which I suggested could go in one corner. That was like lighting a fuse. "A refrigerator in my log room? Not a chance." cried the laird. More plans were drawn up and within days the workmen were wielding their saws and hammers, producing an extension out that back door, of a kitchen, bathroom and bedroom. By a nice chance the back of the fireplace would keep the bathroom cosy. A whole new long list of To-Dos was born and I won't detail the tiles for the kitchen and bathroom floors, the wallboards (obtained in Bancroft a few at a time and held precariously on the roof of the car by helpers' gripping hands), insulation, kitchen shelves, paint by the bucket, board and batten on the outside to blend with the logs. It seemed endless but exciting too and well worth the effort. The story of the next forty years and the friends who came and helped us enjoy our castle (with more additions) would fill a book of its own. Oh yes...not to leave out the whole lovely septic system that had to be installed outside. Through it all I could almost imagine Mr. Wood installed on his cloud casting an approving eye down on the results of his long ago generosity to a dreaming teenager.

Ron's dream cabin finally "chinked" and all together after the war. An ongoing project."

## 11. THE DOCUMENT

It really is true that everyone has a story to tell. I experienced that when I interviewed all those seniors in Napanee for the S.O.S. (Seniors Outreach Services) newsletter, who were convinced their lives had been dull. I count the following part of my past as being if not unique at least very rare. Who ever heard of a financial document being the source of stories? Yet that is the very thing I dug out on my last trip to the attic in better shape than I deserve for not storing it better. The other rarity was that we four orphans without relatives to take us over were in the hands of the government's Official Guardian, McGregor Young K.C. (as was the Document). We never met him but his tenure was without personal prejudice and worked well. Unbelievably the item I noted for him was payment of $8.33 for some court order for Edward...probably the lowest bill ever submitted by any lawyer anywhere!

The said document is legal-sized and dusty brown-covered, with yellowing onion skin pages and only the words "The Canada Trust Company" typed on the cover. Inside, under the date "April 1940", are the detailed closing statements for the estates of Edith I. Dampier (my mother), Sarah Dampier (my paternal grandmother), and L.H.Dampier (my father). The typing was obviously on an old probably Underwood machine. The part that intrigues me most is that this particular statement spans exactly ten very crucial years in my life. My father was buried on my 11th birthday...April 10, 1930, at which time the trusteeship of Canada Trust began. It ended, as Dad's will instructed, on my 21st birthday, April 10, 1940. My three older siblings...Marjorie, Lawrence and Edward, were made to wait until I reached my majority before they received their inheritances. A good plot for a whodunit, hingeing on a fatal accident to me...except that the stakes were very low indeed. Anyway, I'm sure my sister and brothers were much too upright and loving to entertain such a thought. I have carefully kept my copy over the years, dipping into it occasionally, realizing that the memories that some of those seemingly dry-as-bones financial notations bring flooding back are the stuff of which memoirs are made.

Here are a few items that show how memories pop up. The mere fact that the legacy to the four of us was exactly $18,143.82 each over the ten years was unreal. That took care of rent, clothes, tuition and all other necessities for those years.

...There on the first page is Miss Norman, our local visiting dressmaker, in cold December 1930, receiving $7.50 for coming to us and laboring over those scratchy winter dresses, her mouth full of pins. The ones done for Marjorie, still scratchy, I would inherit when she grew out of them.

...Then, on behalf of our future capitalist brother Larry, the treasurer of Ridley College banked $335.75 in 1931 for the whole Lenten term coming up. What would it be in 2013? As eldest son Dad had sent him off to that private school as his British background demanded. Forget other son Ted!

...In January poor Miss Manton, the church organist, received $2.00 for suffering through giving me piano lessons every week that month...ugh! Oh how I hated those sessions. Would that they had been dance sessions where I might have had some fun.

...Then pops out the $5.00 our lawyer Mr. Bixel clocked up for his services. No lawyer would believe that one now.

....Mrs. Daisy Dorothea Pugsley has regular entries of $55.00 for all our monthly board and lodging. She was the rectorr's widow, he having died just after Dad. There are other bills from her, each when we had won an argument.

...Larry ranks first for money spent on clothes and university supplies over the next four years. Ted was low on the totem pole with meager payments like $6.50 to Tip Top Tailors for clothing. So much for a British background if you are the second son!

...I see a dress for Mary, $4.98, at D'Allairds. That's where Mrs. P.'s daughter Connie worked so I got some advantage there. The best place to drag Mrs. P. if I wanted her to buy me something.

...Marjorie scored $2.75 for books at popular Wendell Holmes...not one paperback but all the books she needed that year at University of Western Ontario.

...By way of contrast for Mary there was that controversial bill tendered by Miss B.Birrell on November 12, 1938 for $65.18 for her bridesmaid's dress for Marjorie's wedding that almost was refused by The Guardian for such extravagance. Would that I had saved those 20 yards of soft green chiffon that could be pulled through a ring. Something else I didn't cherish properly.

...Then in December 1938 payment to Bland and Co. in Montreal for Royal Vic uniforms of $44.70 for Mary as that life-changing date of January 31, 1939 fast approached...her entry into a rigorous nurse's training. Those years are a Blog story of their own.

...Regularly from April 1930 to the end of my training I received a monthly allowance of $15.00. That was instead of submitting individual bills. I became the loans banker for my friends who were always broke.

Turning those pages I had to pull myself away from being engulfed in the wealth of remaining items. Back it goes into the attic, more carefully boxed for future reference. It could probably find a place in today's Canada Trust Museum (if they have one!).

## 12. CELEBRATING FEBRUARY 2

For us, celebrating February 2nd has nothing to do with that famous little groundhog Wiarton Willie who always ventures out of his hibernation on that day to let us know how much more winter we must endure. If he sees his shadow we are stuck for another six weeks. I understand he has a rival somewhere down in the States but in Canada we stick with Willie.

There are many memories tucked away among the cobwebs ready to tell my story bur the source herself is still among us...a tiny black nun, Sister Constance S.S.J.D. Surprising to many, The Sisterhood of Saint John the Divine is an Anglican Order and entirely in Canada with headquarters in a lovely recently built convent in north Toronto on the same property as the Rehabilitation Hospital which they had been instrumental in operating. This is Sister's home. On February $2^{nd}$, 2013, a party there marked Sister Constance's $109^{th}$ birthday. That amazing achievement makes her the oldest American residing in this country, a fact that was noted by President Obama when he had the American Ambassador visit her the year she turned 105 and present her with a framed greeting from the President himself.

Her family background is fascinating on its own merits. Constance Murphy's (the name they took in America) family forebears, just a few generations back, had arrived as black slaves from Africa. She never mentioned that part of her history. By the time she was born in 1904 the clan had established itself as leaders in their Afro American community in Baltimore. One grandfather founded and edited "The Afro American" newspaper...the other owned a successful catering business (no lack of sweet treats for growing children). Her father was principal for 50 years of the largest elementary school in the city. Scholarly members practiced law (one teasing brother became a judge). Not to forget several teachers at various levels. What a mind-boggling achievement for that family in a relatively short span of time . She herself graduated from the University of Pennsylvania in 1928, preparing her for the teaching career she practiced for several years. Constance had already become friendly with the "All Saints" sisters in Baltimore and was experiencing a spiritual tug in that direction. However, that connection first led to an entirely different and exciting adventure. Through the Sisters' overseas connections as well as a few friends and relatives Constance and a close friend spent the whole glorious summer of 1929 in Europe...with an itinerary too packed full for our story. Not only that but on their return to teaching they began squirreling away their earnings for a return trip since 1930 would be a year of the Passion play at Oberammergau and another full calendar...mostly of artistic ventures. (In case you are admiring my marvelous memory I am consulting Sister's Memoirs called "Other Little Ships", published in 1997). By now the spiritual tug had become a serious determination within Constance to answer the call to become a Nun. She would have liked to join her friends at "All Saints" but knew it would be better to distance herself from her family. They were strongly against her decision and when she solved her problem by moving to Canada in 1932 they sadly broke off any close connection with her.

After taking her vows our heroine's career included being Head Mistress of a school in Regina, Administrator of the Church Home for the Aged in Toronto, Founder and Chairperson of the Diocesan Committee on the Elderly, member of National and provincial Gerontology Associations in Canada plus several lists of other memberships, awards, publications, honours...culminating in an Honorary Degree from Trinity College, U of T, in 1984. Phew!!! Sister may have been diminutive but she was incredibly strong in mind and spirit. A happy note: surviving members of her family had relented over the years and celebrated with her when she received the Trinity honour.

One of the "elderlies" cared for by Sister at the Church Home had a nephew only known as Mr. Hart. When his aunt died this quiet gentleman met with Sister Constance and informed her that, when he retired, in gratitude for her loving care, he and his Cadillac would be at her disposal every Friday. That promise was kept and the arrival of Sister, riding in state in the back seat, became a weekly sight at her many visitations. Mr. Hart remained faithful to his role as long as Sister could take advantage of it.

My involvement with Sister began with the unlikely fact that I had learned how to make quality-controlled tea essence for large church parish gatherings. After one such successful affair a friend suggested that this was just what they needed at an event for several hundred at St. James Cathedral. I agreed and all went well until I discovered that my good deed had opened a place for me on the Diocesan Committee on the Elderly!! Not liking to offend I toddled along to the next meeting only to find my friend herself had resigned. I also discovered that the committee Chairman was Sister Constance. Unknown to me at that point was the fact that Archbishop Garnsworthy had asked Sister to head up all the diocesan work with the Elderly. "I shall be glad to" Sister had answered, "As long as the Sisters and you allow me to go to Ann Arbor University to get my Master's degree in Gerontology." No matter that she was 70 years old at the time! I found out too soon enough that few had the temerity to refuse her requests. I noted at our next meeting that Sister was quietly surveying all the committee members. At the appropriate moment she announced that I should take her place as Chairperson in her absence. I was too stunned to say a word. The choice I'm sure was due to my having more time available than the others. Forthwith for the next 12 months I did a caretaker job of keeping the committee going on the strength of having attended two committee meetings! Meanwhile tiny Sister Constance in complete black habit and white wimple, always carrying a copious black bag, joined the astonished parade of young people for her classes at the University...much to their amusement until they discovered that she was always perfectly prepared and very articulate. When the year ended the professors allowed as how it was the best class they had ever had. Those young students had to abandon their sloppy ways to prove they were as good as she was!!!

My tenure as Chairman somehow extended to ten years providing experiences I would never otherwise have enjoyed...and not least of all the enduring friendship of an exceptional human being. She considered "The Five", of which I was one, her closest personal friends. Over the years we shared the enjoyment and laughter of a zillion events. They included of course no nonsense involvement in her ongoing programs for her dear elderlies. I cherish the memories of them all.

P.S. - On August 8, 2013, I received a letter from Sister Wilma to inform me that our dear Sister Constance had slipped away the day before "peacefully and quietly" in her $110^{th}$ year. Sister Wilma thanked me for having kept in touch over the years. I had often wished I still lived close by and able to do much more of that. Sister Constance made a huge impact on my life for which I will always be grateful. The funeral was held in St. James Cathedral giving the celebration of her life that she deserved by her hundreds of friends.

Happy picture of Sister Constance and friends (Mary, Kay Steele and Noreen van t'Hof) in Napanee, circa 2005.

Sister Constance

Sister at the Convent on her 105th birthday, receiving the American Ambassador and a letter from United States President Obama

## 13. PICKING UP THE PIECES

It's all very well to be "Random" about my stories...but peering among the joists up in the attic it is obvious that bits and pieces have been missed and are stuffed in the cracks. For instance there are some actual reminders here in the real attic of the post-war days. After clambering up those stairs brother Ted and I always found magic in the lovely mother-of pearl inlaid writing sets in one corner. Dusted off the smooth dark lids would open to reveal slots for pens and nibs and drawers for engraved notepaper and matching envelopes. It would have been fun to have one on our desk and do our homework with scratchy nibs the old-fashioned way. Too bad no stamps remained in those little drawers...probably with the King's profile and a 1 or 2 in the corner. Over there an old bulky trunk or two with brass hinges and locks still held gowns from the Victorian and Edwardian eras that as youngsters we were allowed to handle with care. Now and then they were taken out to hang on display in the windows of Geddes's clothing store downtown. One I loved was long-skirted yellow with a complete layer of intricate black lace underneath with only a few inches showing. Once I was allowed to try on Grandmother Dampier's gray satin wedding gown. Even as a five-year-old I was too chubby to do up the satin-covered buttons that went from hem to neckline at the back. I could close my eyes and envision a fairytale chandelier-lit drawing room with gramma in her finery the belle of the ball!

I realized as I rummaged that there was not a scrap up there to remind me of "Tooie". In my easy chair later I could close my eyes and see that tiny little old lady in dark shiny bombazine and white apron plodding about our house in her carpet slippers as she attempted to perform the duties of a fill-in caregiver for four fractious youngsters. No thanks went her way for the bowls of canned peas swimming in white sauce or the sugared bread and warm milk she considered suitable supper fare for young stomachs. Tooie was our nickname for Susan, an hostler's unmarried daughter in Old London who had in her prime come out from England to be a maid for grandmother Dampier in Canadian London. By the time we knew her in the twenties she was long retired to a tiny room in back street Strathroy to live out her days with meager savings. We did visit her occasionally and she was, even in that isolation, better cared for than most such hired help. No "safety nets" or universal health care or even much compassion in those days.

No account of The Twenties at our place would be complete that didn't include Dad's precious Chev touring car...vintage circa 1924.

Pretty enterprising for a man his age to acquire such a new invention and goodness knows how he learned to drive it. Brought back to original condition just think what a treasure it would be in 2013!!! It's original home was being backed into the old Bogue barn next door and there was practically a business meeting to determine if it should be driven out. How we pestered Dad for a Sunday afternoon jaunt. He would lean back in his rocker and peer up at the sky. The slightest sign of clouds would nix the deal. We learned the importance of that the day we were caught in a rainstorm. Poor Dad in his Sunday suit had to scramble out and try to snap on the isinglass curtains to keep us from being drenched.

    First of course the thing had to be started. Dad would hunker down at the front of the car to locate the place where the crank had to be inserted. He held the awkward gadget with a wooden handle and finally amid much muttering found the metal insert a "Zag" below. Once in place Dad would brace himself and give the thing a mighty turn. It would take several grunting attempts and expletives before there was a roar as the engine went into action. Next came a sprint and climb into the car to work the gas pedal and keep the contraption going. Then, whichever of the four of us were on hand happily climbed in but the adventure had only begun. There was often a puncture of one of the spindly tires that had to be hands-on repaired with a patch on the spot. Hills presented a challenge to which going up backwards was often the only solution. We loved it when we had to get out and help the engine make the grade. I've seen pictures of fashionable ladies wearing hats with veils to keep out the clouds of dust those drives generated but there was no such luxury for dust-covered us. Thirty five was the speed limit on those uneven gravel roads but no chance we would ever exceed that rate. Of course winter meant removing the battery and tires and bedding down the creature in the barn until Spring. Had anyone ventured out in cold weather there were no heaters so a pottery" pig" full of hot water and many lap robes for passengers would be put to use. The windshield could be hand-wiped only with an inefficient rag kept for the purpose. Gas at 15 cents a gallon was no problem and having cars serviced regularly hadn't been invented. Even I could sit on the veranda and name every make of car that drove by…Chevrolet, Plymouth, Ford and Dodge with only one design each made it easy. Mr. Ford had no idea that one day the automobile would "have us by the throat" and turn us into a world on wheels with problems spiralling out of control.

    Ah for those uncomplicated Twenties! Lots has happened since them though that have their own charm and excitement.

## 14. GOOD OLD GOLDEN RULE DAYS!

Adults in the Twenties were still recovering from World War 1 even though the action had been far across the ocean. Our boys had fought and died there and many families bore the scars. At the same time young people felt a breeze of freedom. Gone were the corsets and button boots of pre-war days. I was too young to be a flapper but we watched goggle-eyed as our big sisters bobbed their hair and practiced the Charleston in dresses with drooping waist lines showing silk-stockinged legs and cloche hats pulled down over their heads. The new world came to life but children spent their days at school as they always had. One-room schoolhouses still dotted the countryside and tales of trekking through miles of snow in bitter winter weather clutching school books and lunch to huddle around a wood stove were still common. Strathroy was a metropolis by comparison but school life was still no picnic. Colborne Street Public School was just two doors away from our place (the Bogues in between). It was an unlovely gray two-storey brick building overlooking an uncultivated schoolyard divided in two with a board fence preventing contamination by the opposite sex. I wonder if the Bogues ever objected to the potent odors no doubt floating across to their yard from the "one-holer" toilets housed at the far ends of the two playgrounds? Home being so close we were forbidden to use them...no hardship.

Inside was the other unique smell of strong floorboard cleaner and many infrequently washed bodies. I'm sure there must have been tap water somewhere to wash grubby hands and I have memories of fountains in the hall for drinking. Otherwise I have absolutely no recollection of eating or drinking anything during school hours. Would our pop-pizza-donut-fed young people believe in such deprivation?

Pre-school literally meant staying home and for me that was a boring no-man's land...my sole companion the busy housekeeper. I was shattered when Ted, the last, followed my other siblings out the door. Between us Ted and I plotted a solution. One day I sneaked out with him having told Dad I was playing with a friend and the teacher that I had permission. I can picture those few ecstatic hours as I molded plasticine to my liking at the back of the room. That plus blocks about covered the equipment. Of course our ruse was soon discovered and I returned but to stricter supervision. Brother Larry...ever the organizer ...did take to teaching me letters on our little blackboard after school. The day I achieved the letter "r" was a triumph.

At age five I at last clutched Ted's hand and legally joined the parade of marching legs through that magic door as someone pounded out "God Save the King" on a piano. The Junior classes were two to a room downstairs and the senior grades in the magic upstairs. Very soon I was part of a mixed gang that lasted through all the grades and the names are still engraved on my memory. We were thrilled to get a small slate and marker each to record our lessons. There were holes in the desks for ink bottles. We were never allowed the new-fangled fountain pens since they were considered bad for penmanship…like those endless up and down exercises that filled our slates and later scribblers.

I actually recently re-found my precious autograph book with poems and messages inscribed shakily by my buddies over the years. For example my first beau Billy Buoy wrote on his page: "The thunder roared, The lightning flashed, And all the earth was shaken. A little pig curled up his tail and ran to save his bacon!" How romantic! Early on a cute red-headed girl marched up to me and announced that she knew who I was and we were going to be friends! And so it was with Clara McCandless. The friendship had downs though like when my nose was out of joint seeing her pile of Valentines from the annual box win hands down. How could I compete with those freckles and red curls with my thick glasses and straight hair with zig zag bangs from having Dad put a tie around my head to cut them? Just the same Clara (now Thomas) and I have been friends all the decades since.

Clara and I have tried to find anyone else who spent their first school year in three "Card Classes". No cards existed but it was a kindergarten-like experience, three stepping stones leading to Grade One. Any other "card classers" out there? Of course over the years we had favorite teachers such as Miss Cameron who read us stories Friday afternoons like "Just David", "Secret Garden" and "Tarzan of the Apes."
Seems we were no angels and misbehaved even with her to the extent that she refused to finish the Tarzan book that term and we never did know whether he and Jane ended happily ever after. Miss Newton was our ogre with a dab hand using a slap of the ruler against young palms. How we detested her. Mr. Cuddy was the principal and his favorite ploy was to throw the chalk at an offending head. Sanitation was not on the curriculum. When we had sniffly colds and our handkerchiefs became soggy they were just draped over the floor register to dry. Lacking uninvented Kleenex our immune systems surely took a beating.

Recess was blissful with minimal equipment. In entrance class I got to ring the bell if I could grab it before my rival. The girls' side of the yard had a big shady maple tree where sand made room for hopscotch or a game of the now-forbidden many-pronged jacks with a little ball (hospital shelves have a collection of jacks rescued from childish throats). We did have skipping ropes and could even fly in and out for "double dutch". Huddling under the tree to gossip and giggle was often enough. Whooping and hollering was constant from the boys' side and the occasional ball would come popping over the fence for us to lob back. Too dangerous to snoop there. They did have a teeter totter on that side and when brother Ted sat on it for a visit when he had a cast on a broken wrist he was jolted off by a pull on the other end to suffer a broken second arm. Poor Mrs. H. had to feed and dress the patient until one cast was off.

Entertainment outside the school yard included skating in winter...beginning with tumbling around the local outdoor rink on two-runner bob skates strapped onto our shoes. Later we played crack the whip on regular skates at the indoor rink...until it was banned before we knocked ourselves and other skaters flying. Birthday parties were a rare treat with Pin The Tail on the Donkey a favorite game...and perhaps a bit of Spin the Bottle to add spice. No such thing as gifts since we didn't have that kind of pocket money. The birthday cake was It. Ted and I had one treat that required me riding with him on his bike out to the apple cider factory. They had big presses and let us kneel down and literally slurp up some of the juice still seeping out. There were lots of games for summer evenings...Tappy on the Icebox, Hide and Seek, races of all kinds and the ball even tossed over the house yelling "Annie, Annie aye over!" The unwritten rule was that all the sport ended at eight-o-clock sharp or the family police-Dad would be on the prowl. By then bed was a welcome end to the day. Every kid in town played outside every Spring, Summer and Autumn evening. On my walks in Napanee I noted a meager three or four groups that were not glued to the flashing TV screens and computers inside. But we won't get into that discussion!

This is a good spot to slip in the "stay at home" days. That definitely did not include heavy snowfalls. Snow was a consistent ingredient of winter and plodding through it a given. Our clothes were not as efficiently designed as today to keep us snug so we suffered from chill-blains around our wrists and general cold discomfort. Just like children everywhere we loved it if we had to stay home even if it meant we had a really bad cold. I remember well having my face wrapped in a cloth to try and ease the pain of a throbbing toothache. No antibiotics so the abscess would run its long course. Measles, scarlet fever, mumps, whooping cough, chicken pox, were expected to come in their time. We would duly be quarantined with a sign on the front door for the required length of time. Sometimes treatment required hanging up cloths soaked in carbolic acid to scare away the germs. Getting back to school looked more appealing than itching pox and other discomforts. We vied for the biggest scabs when we were vaccinated against small pox and were warned of the dangers of picking them off.

"School Days" in our case had to include the grade before entrance class because we had to hike across town to the other centre of learning Maitland Street School. In turn their entrance class came to us. This trip made useful the siren used by the furniture factory to mark the starting and finishing work periods…particularly for us the loud blare at twelve noon for the walk home for dinner and one-thirty to be back to our afternoon session. Far from being a chore the trek introduced me to another social pastime. Twos and threes joined up, taking advantage of entertainment en route. The boys shared questionable jokes I never understood and the girls whispered and giggled. The apple-packing shed with bins along both sides on the way through was fair game. Girls' roomy bloomers and the boys' baggy "breeks" could hold a stash of snows, russets, Kings and Spys…just to show our thieving skills since Dad bought apples by the bushel and we just threw out any with a blemish. At the railroad tracks we were forbidden to crawl under the stationary freight cars, which only added to the fun for the braver types who defied the rule. I wasn't even tempted. Even further along there was a deserted factory and shying stones at the windows a good sport. It lost its glamour for me when I was caught and had to donate several weeks allowance to pay for my sins. That allowance already had to go to the Penny Bank run by the school…ten cents every week. To digress…it was a great payoff when my savings contributed the greater part of money to buy me a fur coat some years later. A lesson learned.

Oh yes…and to end the journey we had to pass a pile of rotting corn at another wayside factory. That meant holding our noses and running like mad to the school door. The goal was worth it though since we girls were all in love with our handsome young teacher. One of his favorite pastimes was to find any chestnuts that had been secreted in errant pockets and eat them in front of us! He betrayed us further by getting married at the end of our year!

It's a story that wends its way through my childhood and still conjures up a series of pictures for me to smile over as I stretch out in my easy chair for my daily rest hour.

Clara and Mary...lifelong friends...circa 1980.

## 15. HOLIDAYS AWAY FROM HOME

It's the easy chair today for relaxing and enjoying summer memories...a nostalgic ramble rather than an exciting journey. Hopefully these won't get away from me like The Good Old Golden Rule Days did. I can't promise...new bits may again keep popping up, demanding attention. As a start...the jump for joy at leaving school each year at the end of June soon wore off...we longed for the bliss of the beach. Families in Western Ontario split between Lake Huron and Lake Erie for their respite. Dad's choice was a month at Grand Bend on Lake Huron. I haven't been back in many years but hear that it is now a busy, crowded, somewhat raucous modern resort. Back then it was a quiet main street of small shops and booths and a couple of clapboard hotels with streets of cottages branching off into the woods. Dad's aim was to have his band of heathens able to amuse themselves, leaving him to a well-earned rest. In July, having announced the plan ("When do we leave Dad?", " Please hurry up Dad!") the Chev was finally loaded with our simple gear including baggy cotton bathing suits that clung to wet skin...and a little pail and shovel for me as I recall. We piled in and Dad's grim efforts with the crank burst us into action. Forty miles of gravel at maybe 25 miles an hour stretched ahead (hopefully without punctures) and it seemed endless. We tried seeing who could spot the most white horses in the fields (white horses?)...or played games of "I spy". Or there was who could spot the most license plates from the States. Those were low dollar days so good for tourists. And of course frequent noisy squabbles (Daddy...Larry punched me!). When we finally came to the spot where a big red barn looked as though it was in the middle of the road we could shout with glee. We knew our trip was about over.

My first recollection is of the white-painted Lakeshore Hotel (long gone) right at the beach, its second floor enveloped in a veranda full of mostly occupied slatted chairs. That summer I was four and managed to contract measles and had to be taken back to the hospital in Strathroy amid multi tears. The dangers of that disease were not yet known. The memory there is that the hospital was full and also under construction for an addition and I was terrified that my bed at the end of the hall would fall over the open abyss! Another year just Ted and I were in tow and we stayed at the Bossenberry Hotel further up the street. Ted was entranced by the owner's curly-haired daughter, referred to as "Bummy Bossenberry" so was lost to me as a playmate. I remember being overawed by the large bright dining room full of white-clothed tables. I was even allowed to ring the bell for the meals. Ever hungry I have a mental picture of eating both my 2 poached eggs and one from Dad plus several pieces of butter soggy toast at breakfast...what bliss. I've never forgotten though that a couple of observant ladies had a look with disapproval at my hands as I lolled in a veranda chair. My grubby nails needed not only cleaning but clipping and my mentors proceeded to do it. Not something poor harassed Dad would notice. Of course we spent many happy hours on the sandy beach building castles and jumping into the (to me) always frigid water. Already not seeing well and having brothers who pushed me under until I was spluttering made me terrified of the water and delayed my learning to swim for several years. There is a real photo of me standing shyly in the lake in my clingy cotton suit. Close to the lakeshore there was a big pavilion for dancing...out of limits for us. That didn't prevent us from sneaking in after bed-time to watch the bodies in the exotic lights dancing to the rhythmic band music. Oh to be grown up.

Dad's next choice was a pink clapboard cottage on one of the streets back from the lake. Mrs.H., our trusty housekeeper, came along by then to cook meals and care for him in this rather primitive rental. Dad had developed leg ulcers and sat propped up on the porch most of the day. That left the lot of us roaming at will through the waving beach grasses and over the dunes...an ideal setup for Hide and Seek. One day brother Larry tried his hand at rolling grass in paper and not only smoking it but enticing us to do the same! His hacking and turning red in the face put us off that one. Sun screen was a term of the future. We just baked in the sun until we were not only red but had big water blisters on our backs. I wince even now to report that the boys would chase the girls to poke and burst them as we howled It's a wonder we didn't get blood-poisoning. Actually the size and extent of the damage became a matter of honor!

That summer we met up with the Chesham gang...Fred the eldest already had the makings of the soldier he became. Hemmie (Evelyn) my age and sister Marion a year younger were most attractive and bubbling with fun and good spirits. They lived in London but we had known them in Strathroy where they visited their grandmother Mrs. De Jay. Back then we had been rung in as fitting playmates for the visitors. In Grand Bend they were stranded with the adults (mother and grandmother )too and were delighted to join our harum-scarum gang, ranging over the sandy dunes and along the main street scattered with food booths. Little did we girls think that our lives would be joined in lifelong bonds of friendship some years later when we met at Western University in London the day we all enrolled in the B.Sc. In Nursing course. In those Twenties we were content just to spend one happy roving day after another...nipping back for cookies and milk at the

Chesham menage.  That main drag in Grand Bend did provide Hemmie with the means to tease me in the years to come as having taught her how to steal by snitching apples or snacks from one of the booths and showing her how.

There was an area of more affluent cottagers further north called Oakwood…separated from the hoy-polloy by a wire fence.  Living with The Countess (Mrs.Pugsley) while in High School I summered in her roomy brown-stained shingle-covered cottage there.  It was a mixed blessing.  I really wanted to go to the YWCA camp Orendaga as my sister had done and like all my friends were doing now.  For some unknown reason Mrs.P. wouldn't let me.  Her daughters, Marg and Connie, were much older and on the prowl for male company.  Alone I would step over their sunning bodies and walk through the edge of the water the mile to the pier in town and back again.  Our beach was deep and having no beach shoes I would run like mad and then sit down and wave my feet in the air to cool them off.  By the end of the summer my soles were leathery and had a split down the middle.  The real bane of my existence though was the poison ivy that plagued me each year.  Mrs. P. had not learned that burning the plants only released the oil to settle on sensitive skin.  Altogether I was an ungrateful camper and I would sing to myself the camp song my sister had taught me:

> *Oh I walked into Aylmer and I walked around the block*
> *And I walked right into a donut shop*
> *I took a donut out of the grease*
> *And I handed the lady a 5-cent piece*
> *Oh she looked at the nickel and she looked at me*
> *And she said this nickel's no good to me*
> *There's a hole in the middle and it goes right thru*
> *Says I…There's a hole in the donut too!!*
> *Shave and a haircut….two bits!!!*

That was my teenage dirge of longing for a life of my own!

## 16. SCHOOL IS STILL OUT

Sure enough. A climb to the attic and a couple of dust balls were bouncing toward me in a frenzy. The winner to be recorded first was my one and only venture onto a farm...albeit a "gentleman's" version. It came about at our house in Strathroy on April $10^{th}$, 1930. I have two reasons for remembering that date so accurately. It was my eleventh birthday which was not being celebrated. It was also the day of my father's funeral and as I hung about in the Spring sunshine I could see the gathering of somber adults dressed in black on our front veranda. I had been barred from attending the funeral as being too young...a sad mistake I came to believe since it was my only chance at some kind of closure for the staggering loss of my only beloved remaining parent. Among those on hand was a middle-aged couple, Jim and Marg Smith. Marg was one of the progeny of Archbishop David Williams of the Anglican Diocese of Huron...a handsome white-haired Welshman. Her four siblings filled the accepted requirement of clergy young to be "holy" terrors...but sensible Marg had married the City of London engineer Jim Smith. The connection that had brought the couple to this sad event was that Dad's first wife Louise Burwell had been a sister of the Archbishop's wife. Jim and Marg owned a farm on Base Line Road outside London with their daughter "Sis" about my age. They had most kindly decided to offer a month's vacation to the youngest of the newly created orphans. So that day they did and the offer was duly accepted by the powers that be.

Fast forward to July and Mary in her best cotton dress standing nervously clutching her suitcase when Uncle Jim chugged up to Mrs. Pugsley's apartment...now my home. Bad enough to be going off all alone but a "farm" was a scary prospect for an ignorant eleven-year-old townie. My sole experience with farms was those drives in the Chev past vast fields, big old farmhouses and barnyards filled with mooing cows and/or stomping horses, scratching chickens and pigs snuffling in the mud. What fun was there for a pre-teen in a place like that? Sensing my panic Uncle Jim, a gentle soft-spoken man, patted my head, "Don't worry now...you'll soon see" he assured me. And soon I did as we slowed down and turned into a winding driveway leading to an attractive stone house surrounded by clipped lawns. A flower garden on one side overflowed with colorful blooms, the perfume of sweet peas and roses wafting from their trellises. On the other side stretched rows of vegetables including waving corn. Near the house a tree spread its limbs loaded with its crop of bright red cherries. A moo did come from the neat barn behind and a horse's whinny directed me to his head peering out of a stall. I was agape but best of all was the sight of plump Aunt Marg beaming a welcome from the doorway while Sis peeked shyly from behind her. With hugs all round my fears evaporated.

Highlights of my farm vacation:

...At first "Sis", with whom I spent most of my time, was a mixed blessing. She was a pretty dark-haired girl but mentally handicapped and unable to read and write or do many quite simple chores without supervision...at first a real drag for me. After a bit I learned to help her. It felt good and we soon became friends.. Besides, she knew every nook and cranny of that farm and was wonderful with the animals. Sis was the only one who could handle the unschooled mare Sparky and would coax her and chase her across the field, finally jumping on bareback for a wild ride while I cheered. When Sis milked the cow it never kicked over the pail as it did when I tried. The dog and cats were her domain as well.

...Aunt Marg was a super cook and sent Sis and me out to battle the robins for those cherries. Swishing them away with a towel while filling our pail was hard work but worth the effort that night when a yummy cherry cake came out of the oven.

...I suspect that giving each of us a pail to tie around our waist and sending us out to the wild raspberry patches was Aunt Marg's way of getting a little peace. Mosquito swatting was part of the deal. I soon learned to ignore Sis eating every berry she picked. I'd keep going until I had enough to top up her pail before we headed home in the afternoon heat.

...That was when we would rush to pull on our bathing suits and head for our afternoon swim. I guess I forgot to tell you that engineer Uncle Jim had used his expertise to have a farm pond in a nearby field emptied and cleaned out with a layer of gravel installed instead of the previous mucky bottom. Refilled and with a diving board it was complete. Getting there meant carefully bypassing the thistles and also those round piles Sis forgot to warn me about and hooted loudly when I stepped right into one! Sis hit the water like a seal but I had yet to learn to swim...a problem Uncle Jim solved by coaxing me to jump from the diving board into the shallow water...except that it was over my head. He just laughed when I surfaced spluttering and navigating with flailing arms and legs enough to get to shore. Cruel but effective and he was there if I needed him. Diving came with my second farm summer.

...I actually learned to like the warm milk as it came from "Bossy" each morning. The cream was saved to use in the butter churn...a primitive hand-turned affair that made my arms ache. We took turns and were delighted when the butter blobs appeared.. I liked best when I was sent out to bring in corn for the next meal...oh how sweet were those cobs rolled in that butter!

…A dividend that had nothing to do with farming was Aunt Marg teaching me to knit and follow a pattern. A useful skill and I was short of that kind of training.

…The one thing I didn't learn during that blissful month was any kind of farming. What a compassionate gift that holiday was when I needed it most.

## 17. BRO LARRY HITS HIS STRIDE

Just musing a bit in the easy chair, a memory has surfaced that for once belongs to someone else..."Bro" Larry. Lacking all those bits that I always add to my own events this should be a short story for a change. You may have gathered from previous comments that Larry was from the beginning a strong-minded bossy boy. Quiet Ted being just a year younger never got out from under that strong personality. Nor did Larry have any compunctions about poking and teasing his baby sister and even dropping her dolls down the stair well. So, I disliked him profoundly then...but in adulthood loved him dearly.

One of the few amenities in our small town was a Boy Scout Troop (no counterpart for girls). A worldwide Scouting event was planned for 1929 in England to celebrate the 50$^{th}$ Anniversary of the movement begun by Baden-Powell. Every scouting district was to choose a King Scout to be its representative at the two-week-long camp housing thousands of young people. Strathroy was only one part of the larger troop centred in the city of London, Ontario. The first horrendous hurdle was to acquire a King Scout Badge. Then the applicants had to pass a list of rigorous tests to prove they were the best of the best.

You've probably guessed it...Bro Larry achieved not only the badge but the vote to be the rep. His family and Strathroy as a whole were stunned and to this day we have no idea how he achieved it. I will say that it was a forewarning of many unlikely achievements in his future...including a stint as President of the Boy Scouts of Canada. For now this was enough to absorb.

Dad of course was proud of his eldest and managed the necessary pocket funds. It was an exuberant assembly that gathered at the little station to see him off. He would join his trip companions in Halifax to board the Lusitania and sail off for Great Britain and the greater adventure. I remind you now that we are talking about 1929. We would have no contact of any kind from Larry until he emerged again from the train at our station on his return. Here are just a few things that we eventually learned:

...On the trip over someone talked him into eating some tripe to prevent sea sickness and he was grossly ill.

...Rain turned the enormous camping grounds into a muddy morass.

...He met a grand bunch of guys and the English people treated them like kings.

The exit from the train on the return trip said it all. Larry swung down from the car completely garbed in a Scottish kilt and all the trimmings. He was an instant celebrity and I remember well his arriving in my class at school in full kit to twirl in the kilt and relate his adventures. This claim to fame in no way lessened Dad's fury when he discovered that his son no longer owned a decent suit of clothes since he had swapped everything he had with him for the kilt.

One thing I don't recollect is any sign of repentance on the part of the young hero.

### 18. BRUCE BEACH THE BEST

This little ball of dust is a bit ahead of himself but still fills the bill of a final "School is Out". This time it was Central Collegiate in London Ontario. My "Girl Gang" was close to the end of its teens and the vacations those last two years became a bit of a "Rite of Passage" for us. The real world was waiting in the wings but for those two summers we were in charge and did as we liked for the first time. It was Max (short for Maxine) who dreamed up the whole idea. I had met her the year I moved to London and started at Central. The other four friends became classmates for the following four years. No "Bios" of them though since that's not what this is all about.

Max had enjoyed some time at a friend's cottage in Kincardine on Lake Huron. "There's a great little resort about 5 miles down the lake with neat cottages for rent" she enthused. "Why don't we try and get one and go for a month on our own?" It was a blockbuster idea and there was not a dissenting voice in the group. No need for the details...renting the cottage, parental permission, car transportation etc. It was actually amazing in those more disciplined times that the exciting goal was achieved. Even Mrs. Pugsley couldn't refuse with so many assenting parents. Come July of 1938 the caravan took off for the one-storey clapboard dream house sitting on a pebbly beach that was costing us all of $60 for the entire 4-weeks. As the cars disappeared back down the road we hugged each other and whooped for joy. Unbelievable!

The gray painted building was cubby-holed into four bedrooms around a living room and backed by a kitchen and dining room...all airily open above. A somewhat drunken veranda stretched across the front. The teenagers of year 2013 would surely find what follows hard to believe. For cooking the kitchen contained an erratic wood stove. Our untutored struggles to get a fire going usually enveloped us in eye-stinging smoke before we had success. The "facilities" were in a matching gray wood shed out back. The only entertainment gizmo at hand was a Victrola which dear Elizabeth Robinson had the wit to bring along. She was our source of records and all the words to our favorite songs. Easy to carry it out to the beach and crank it up as we lounged on our towels singing and clapping to the beat. Having no radio, phone, TV, cell phones or computers put us personally in charge of the action. And by the way, no car, bicycle or bus...just shanks mare all the way. Consensus mostly ruled rather than agreement. Having no store or any pop or snack machines we settled for our own crackers and cookies.

The only feast I remember was when we cooked the oatmeal for breakfast one evening and then were so starved we ate it out on the beach under the stars before bed! Piles of pancakes and syrup were popular fare. No such thing as a barbecue. We took turns preparing meals...that is to say the designated couple argued their way through the suggested menu. Our own group did play bridge about which we knew little but wrangled over a lot. There were lots of other young holidayers of both sexes on hand and the expanse of lake water for swimming, some balls for beach games and lots of space for races provided all the sport we needed. There was plenty of rowdy action. Someone had even produced what passed for a mini golf course with sand greens to putt around on. Extant somewhere is a postcard graced with a photo of the eight lovelies in residence at that time crowded on to our only bench. Who needs chairs?

So...how about food for unlimited teenage appetites and where did it come from? We had brought starter provisions with us and a friendly young Kincardine man with a small panel truck soon appeared at our door and once a week thereafter. He took the list we had pored over the night before. Two days later the truck came belting back through the woods with our supplies. One bill survives...the hand-written sheet was full and the total cost a bit over four dollars. (My expenses for the whole month all-inclusive were $40) Our brash young driver offered one day to take some of us to visit Kincardine. He did neglect to add that he also planned to try and beat a friend, also at the wheel of a truck, on the dash over a primitive track to town. We piled into the back, the door was closed and in the pitch dark we were treated to a wild tossing about like bags of hay as the boys careered through the trees. Happily we only suffered bruises and one pair of shattered glasses (glasses don't do that anymore). As for our eating habits and meals be in no doubt...food was a major factor in our lives and we made sure we had plenty of it, wild rides or not!

Behavior-wise we mostly lived up to our families' trust in us. The mores of 1938 were unbelievably far from those of 2013. None of the local boys ever even tried to come into the cottage although cute red-headed Marie was the most popular in our beach and other games. If there was any hanky panky I never knew it. Yes...we puffed at an occasional cigarette from the one package that someone had brought with them (my one recollection is that Turrets were a cent each) since we certainly would never have put them on the grocery list. These had to be hidden the time a car arrived to pay us a visit...our only sighting of family for the whole month. There was no beer or alcohol of any kind to be seen and we had never heard of drugs as a pastime. And believe it or not...a couple of times a church group held a service in the field behind us on a Sunday and most of us happily attended! No...I'm not making it up and namby-pambies we were not. We were just part of the times.

There were few glitches.  Barb Thompson was a thorn in our flesh for being bossy and liking to rise too early and turn the music up high as she quite unnecessarily swept the living room causing imprecations from the would be sleepers.  One day Marion Chesham was a casualty to sunburn so severe that she lay starkers on the floor for hours while we kept dousing her with cold tea to ease her flaming flesh!!!  Mostly camaraderie reigned.

Looking back we did learn a lot about getting along with a mix of temperaments and how to run our own affairs.  But that was secondary.  Most of all those carefree two months took the "School is Out" prize.  Without a doubt "Bruce Beach *was* The Best".

## 19. THE FUTURE BECKONS

    I like it when the stories are about other people but they do tend mostly to involve the twists and turns of my own life since that is what fills my memory bank.  So it is with the next trip through some crucial years...even though lots of other people were woven into them.
    At the time I didn't realize what a "quantum leap" my life was going to take after that last ideal teenage vacation at Bruce Beach.  I abandoned the attic and its dust balls and turned to old pictures and mementos to bring those years back to life.  But what plans did I have back then for the future?  A big gap was soon obvious...no parents to turn to.  I know...young people usually ignore adult advice anyway but it does sew seeds and there's a lot for a young head to get around.  First of all my eye specialist mistakenly felt that my short-sightedness ruled out four years of University...an old fashioned myth.  I knew I didn't have what it takes to be a scholar like my friend Clara and there were few other choices.  What I didn't realize (would a parent have twigged?) was that my good exam papers pointed straight at some kind of writing career like journalism.  No such course existed at Western yet but there always had been learning on the job.  Pounding the streets night and day with a notebook and camera in search of a story?  Yikes!  No gumption for that one.  My sister was marrying the publisher of the London Free press and Walter Blackburn  had noted my aptitude with words.  Taking in a family member was a strict NoNo though so he avoided what they called nepotism and I lost a golden opportunity.  Writing...at least as a career ...was on the shelf.
    Then one day like an omen out of the blue I received a postcard with an aerial view of Royal Victoria Hospital, Montreal...a handsome castle-like, turreted edifice on the slopes of Mount Royal...a romantic vista for a small-town girl.  The sender was in training there.  In spite of a mother and aunt who had been nurses I had never considered that route.  But why not?  Western had a B.Sc.N. degree course in nursing that was the ideal answer.  I jumped at the chance in spite of "cautionary tales" about the hazards ahead from a few experienced souls   I was on a roll and brooked no roadblocks.  And maybe wasn't  I more than ready to get out from under the eagle eye of landlady Mrs.P.?  I applied to Royal Vic and was accepted.  The prelims were set in motion.
    I still think Western has one of the loveliest campus settings possible...approached by a winding road crossing a Brigadoon-like bridge, then on up the hill to the gray stone Arts building on its crest,

crowned with a tower...all in a setting of rolling green lawns. To the right was the matching Science building and behind it the Lawson Library completing the 1937 set-up. There were no residences. Now it is a given to get lost in the warren of buildings and streets that have grown up. Student residences line the approaching driveway. Back then it was a small friendly young campus.

Fate stepped right along with me the day I walked into the Arts building for the first time. Joining the lineup of registrants along with faithful friend Max who had made the same choice as I had my eyes popped! There just ahead was none other than pretty auburn-haired Hemmie Chesham whom I had seldom seen since our pre-teen play times in Strathroy and Grand Bend. With her was her friend a real statuesque beauty, Bea Moore. Hard to believe we were all heading in the same direction. The chemistry among the four of us was almost instant.

It will help to know the B.Sc.N. program. The first year would be spent at the university between the Arts College and the Science building. The second year until the end of December concentrated on the science subjects required by the upcoming nurses course. Our problem was to be accepted by one of the hospitals that would then allow students into their regular three-year program while letting them depart three months ahead of time to return for their final year at university. That turreted building on the postcard turned out to be our mutual goal. Max, Hemmie and I had already applied in the prelims and been accepted but there was some nail-biting before Bea overcame her late application and joined us. There was great joy the day her acceptance arrived and the new foursome became a reality.

First came a taste of pleasant college life. Two pictures stand out in my cache. One took place in one of those large sloping tiered classrooms where we had a session just before lunch each day. I didn't know that I had hypoglycemia (shortage of sugar) and should always have a candy or cookie on hand in case of delayed meals. At 11:30 on the dot my stomach would begin to complain much to the hilarity of the classmates close by and my humiliation. I never learned so it was a regular hysterical event. The other was of George my very own once-was rabbit who now resided in a pail of obnoxious formaldehyde waiting for me to operate on some part of him in each lab session. By year's end he was a spine with a tail and I bid him a happy farewell. It was pleasant between classes to visit Room 4 in the Arts building where bridge games were in constant rotation for available players. There we met chipper little Jane Maclean and dark-haired talkative Dorothy Dunn...little knowing how important they would be to us some day. There were rugby games in the Little stadium where we could watch the Mustangs (including Clara McCandless's already beau Morley Thomas) join the piles of arms and legs. And tennis to play on the clay courts and classes to skip for a good movie.

I was delighted to make contact with Clara, now an attractive redhead, who had, not surprisingly, won a scholarship at Strath Collegiate and was in Honors English. I admit some resentment that somebody so smart should also be so darned pretty! More surprising was that she lived upstairs in the same building as the apartment I shared with Mrs. Pugsley and her girls. Clara was looking after a pre-school boy I can only describe as a brat, in order to earn much-needed cash. She and I, as ever full of talk and laughter, would set out each day to walk the couple of miles to classes, usually successful in thumbing a ride up Richmond Street. Foul play was not a factor with the kind local drivers. The time slipped pleasantly by.

Happily after classes ended at the end of December that second year we had a few weeks to catch our breath and prepare for our due date at R.V.H. of January 31, 1939. Immersed in our own plans we were mostly unaffected by the grinding Depression of those Thirties or of Hitler and the looming threat of war. We were a naïve lot too without a clue about the events we had set in motion or what their impact would be on our lives. For those happily euphoric last weeks we were in a whirlwind of preparations mixed with farewell entertaining. The London Free Press featured pictures of the Famous Four on the social page. My recently married sister Marjorie threw a splendid luncheon and I can still taste the yummy ginger snap and whipped cream concoction her cook Bessie produced to top it off. A fog of other gatherings kept us on the hop in between being measured up, down and around for uniforms ordered from Bland and Company in Montreal (skirts 11 inches from the floor no more no less please). Other gathered gear on the list included a scratchy wool blanket, a striped drill laundry bag, black oxfords and hose, down to the last detail of low fashion under apparel. All would be sent ahead in our steamer trunks. Nobody born in the last 50 years would know what in heavens name that monster was. No light luggage on wheels or easy drip drys eased the way.

At train time on a frosty January 30 the somewhat subdued celebrities gathered at the London station…sporting colorful farewell corsages amid a crowd of hugging relatives and friends…more like starlets on the way to Hollywood than probationers heading for nursing boot camp! A sea of waving hands and suddenly we were on our way. The next tableau is double-etched on my mind. Reality struck us dumb as we stood and looked at one another. Then we solemnly shook hands and vowed that…if we all made it through the next almost three years…we would have the biggest party celebration Royal Vic had ever seen!!!

A good point to pause and wait for a sequel?

An early snap through the plane window of Niagara Falls...circa 1950's.

The castle-like postcard that led me up the mountain in 1939
Royal Victoria Hospital, Montreal.

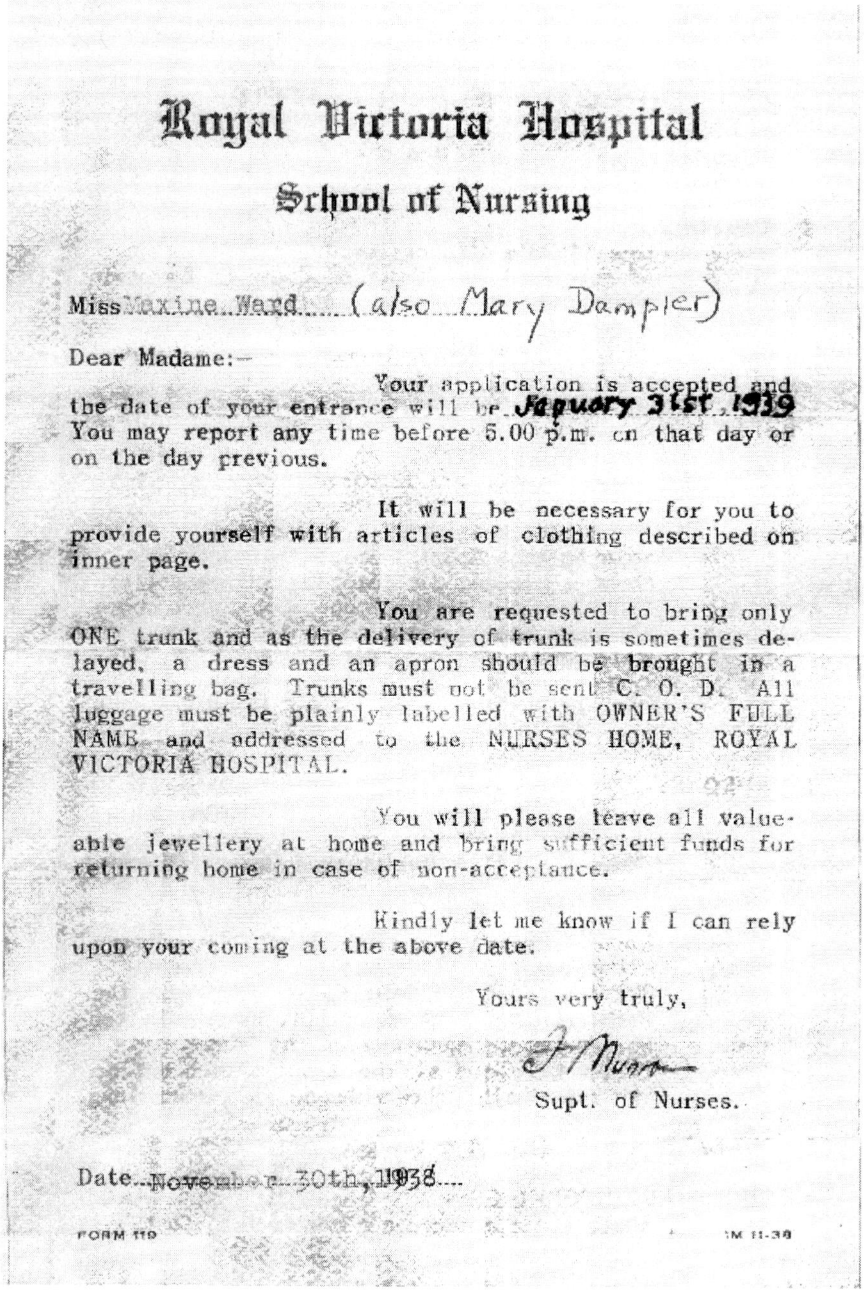

# Royal Victoria Hospital
## School of Nursing

Miss Maxine Ward (also Mary Dampier)

Dear Madame:—

Your application is accepted and the date of your entrance will be **January 31st, 1939**. You may report any time before 5.00 p.m. on that day or on the day previous.

It will be necessary for you to provide yourself with articles of clothing described on inner page.

You are requested to bring only ONE trunk and as the delivery of trunk is sometimes delayed, a dress and an apron should be brought in a travelling bag. Trunks must not be sent C. O. D. All luggage must be plainly labelled with OWNER'S FULL NAME and addressed to the NURSES HOME, ROYAL VICTORIA HOSPITAL.

You will please leave all valueable jewellery at home and bring sufficient funds for returning home in case of non-acceptance.

Kindly let me know if I can rely upon your coming at the above date.

Yours very truly,

F. Nunn

Supt. of Nurses.

Date November 30th, 1938

FORM 119

Letter of acceptance to Royal Victoria Hospital, November 1938

Wedding of the year in London, Ontario, November 9, 1938. Walter Blackburn, Publisher of the London Free Press and Marjorie Dampier. Bridesmaid Mary shown behind.

## 20. INSIDE THE CASTLE

A musing session in the easy chair is called for. For instance, not all my stories stand on their own. Some are mini-sized but still stories...parts of a phase of my life that covers a period of time. They also showcase world events and the huge differences in every aspect of life then and now. The next round is of my nursing "phase" . "The Future Beckons" was really the beginning of it. Enough of the easy chair...here goes.

The bridges were burned and the party was over for the now Subdued Four. Our train pulled into the Bonaventure Station in Montreal after an overnight trip. That red brick colossus with its array of tracks bringing in a constant flow of snorting engines is now long gone. Planes flying overhead into several airports have reduced the flow to a trickle of modern engines lacking the old glamour. The city itself at that time wasn't a problem for English-speaking visitors since the street signs and shops were all still in their familiar language. One unchanging factor remained. The snow was deep and it was a typical frigid Montreal winter morning as we clutched our hand luggage and faced our first venture...the climb on foot through the snow up to the Windsor Hotel for a hot breakfast. As we trudged along how grateful I was to snuggle down into my new muskrat coat...and even more grateful that I had been forced to save $90 in penny bank donations over my school years in Strathroy. Thanks too to Mr. McGregor Young K.C., the Official Guardian, for financing the remaining $30 needed to make it mine. Our final treat included a cab ride for the last leg of the trip up the mountain to R.V.H.

Unlike the fairylike version on my postcard the massive gray stone edifice that came into view through the cab's window was indeed fearsome. The driveway wound up one side to the top of the iron staircase that led down to the door of the adjoining nurses' residence soon to be all too familiar. Safely delivered inside we stared in astonishment at the bright blue hairdo on the prim matron in starched white at the reception desk. We were brusquely dispatched by a minion to out rooms upstairs...Hemmie and I in one and Max and Bea in another nearby. The rest of that day we spent nervously absorbing the lengthy list of Dos and Don'ts that would order our days from then on. In a matter of minutes control of our lives had passed into other hands. Later we would explore the McGill campus spread out below Pine Avenue down to Sherbrooke and the road that wound upward around the mountain to where the lights on the huge cross each night beamed down on the city below.

One fact was soon clear...a hierarchy left over from the Dark Ages still ruled here.   Probationers (Probies for short) were the lowest of the low on the nursing totem pole.   Even students only 6 months ahead came first through a door, into an elevator, getting a seat in the dining room.   We stood if a doctor entered the room and he (no she's there) got to enter the door or elevator first.   We didn't bow to them but next thing to it.  The word gentleman had been shelved.  The get up bell was hand-carried by a rustling figure through the halls at 6 a.m...roll call was at 6:30...classes at 7.   Roll call was alphabetical so the day that both Chesham and Dampier were late led to the bell nurse entering right into our room the next day and scaring the daylights out of us.   A sure cure for the tardy!   I can hear still the rustle of dozens of starched aprons as the bodies scooted down the halls.   Probie classes began immediately next day...farewell to the free-wheeling co-ed life.   One could actually be stood in the corner for having shifted one's glance away from the gimlet-eyed lecturer.  The Head Teaching Nurse Miss Crawford was not above causing tears to flow from a victim being disciplined.  There were no classes on the weekend so we looked forward to a break. Whoops...there was a break alright...for the staff nurses whom we would replace.  We began by rubbing faceless backs and moved on to other caretaker ward jobs.   Oh yes...those lovely long wings on my Disneyland building were 52-bed wards and the towers at the end housed the bed pans.   Re time off...we had a half day a week.   That was improved later by letting us off after only 3 hours labour.  Sundays we had 10 to 3 free (presumably to go to church which we often did) or got a three off. .   On night duty which began at 7 p.m. our night off was until 11 p.m. so we worked only 8 hours that night...a really exhausting posting.  My time clock never did switch over on night duty.    I slept poorly during the day and at night when I sat doing charts my head would hit the desk with a thud.  And somehow I resented having to keep to a whisper throughout the night.   Slave labour by any standards.   At night all in by 10 p.m. except once a month 12 p.m.  That became two so-called  late leaves  a month  the second year and  three the final one. We soon learned that the courageous found ways to slip in a window or get help from a pal but we had no stomach for that.

As Probies we soon began to miss members of our class of 60 every few days.   Without warning and for reasons we never knew they were gone.   The class was close to in half by the time our probie days ended and we felt safe.  I still smile at one snapshot of us up on the residence roof the day we got our hard-won caps and bibs, wielding mops and brooms as emblems of our graduation as "skivvies"!  Now the wards were full time...but still with classes sandwiched into our time off making for 12 -hour days.

I can't resist some statistics.  1. We went from that fateful January 31, 1939 to February 4, 1940 (our first holidays), without one complete day or night off.  2. Then there was Christmas of that first year of being away from home (I did shed tears as I lugged those bed pans).  We were invited out for Christmas dinner with friends.  I was on night duty so had slept the day before until 3 p.m...then worked all night.  A quick change and we all made tracks for the friend's abode for fun and feasting.  Then we returned Christmas evening to work all night again and get to bed the next morning about 9...by my calculations 42 hours without sleep.  My only real memory of that marathon is of having my eyes reduced to slits!  3. Both my brothers were married that first year and I was not allowed to attend...bridesmaid or not.

I do think the background facts were needed...but our next Nursing Phase chapter will deal with our own more "storyfied" experiences...fun and otherwise.

## 21. LEARNING TO LIVE A NEW LIFE

An exciting event for our whole country was the arrival in the summer of 1939 on our shores of the recently crowned King George VI and his delightful radiant Queen Elizabeth. We young people had lived through the loss of George V who had been "our" King whom we thought would live forever. We would miss his Christmas messages. A vivid broadcast memory was on the day of the funeral. Though the streets were packed with mourners there was only an eerie silence save for the clop clop of the horses feet as they pulled the coffin through the streets of London. The accession of the playboy Prince of Wales as Edward VIII hadn't lasted long. We were glued to our radios this time to hear his emotional abdication speech. He had given up the throne in favour of marrying the American divorcee Mrs. Simpson. Hence his brother the Duke of York became a reluctant George VI. This visit to Canada was a happy respite for us all from Hitler's ranting and threats of war. The royal couple were slated to drive in an open car up University Avenue and on between the hospital and the Neurological Institute into Molson Stadium for a welcoming ceremony. Special bleachers had been built for us providing a close sighting both in and out. We were entranced by the Queen in her signature bright blue costume smiling and waving seemingly to us. The King was there of course but drew little of our notice. I was wearing the short handsome red-lined wool cape we had been issued. Sadly it is long gone no one knows where.

A few months later on the morning of September 1$^{st}$ we were as usual hurrying down the stairs to check for any new postings on the bulletin board when we froze in our tracks to see in bold black print..."CANADA AT WAR WITH GERMANY". Radio was our sole source and we had been aware of Chamberlain's attempt to avoid war by his negotiations with Hitler at Munich. But this stark reality was proof of his failure. Soon Churchill's booming voice would regularly broadcast the encouragement needed during the four years ahead.

Personal effects of the war came immediately. A favorite eatery for us on St Catharine's Street on our day off was the Hoffbrau...home of mouth-watering wieners and sauerkraut. September 2 it was gone as though it had never been. Also we recently had enjoyed a champagne birthday party for our classmate Elspeth Geiger at her parents' handsome home when she turned 21. The family was immediately interned we knew not where. Elspeth was allowed to continue her training. After the war she achieved her doctorate at Columbia University in New York and became the Superintendent at Sick Children's Hospital in Toronto. I had taken a year of German in High School but learned later that it was immediately discontinued. In order to be protected from possible danger the innocent were punished as well as the suspect.

    The newest member of our foursome, Bea Moore, was our "femme fatale"...tall and lovely and where the opposite sex was concerned like honey is to Winnie the Pooh. Having experienced this all her life Bea ignored it and preferred the company of her buddies. During our first year she received a dozen lovely roses on the same date of every month from a pining swain back home. Another beau, Bill Cameron, was interning at Montreal General. Having booked a date handsome Bill would arrive as scheduled. Bea would be informed through the intercom we had in our rooms. Usually she would not even have removed her uniform to say nothing of having the needed shower. Of course no men allowed upstairs so hopefully Bill had something to read as he warmed a chair downstairs. From our point of view his greatest attraction was an ancient roadster dubbed "Grumble Guts". It had the look of expiring at any moment. On several occasions he loaned it to Bea for an excursion. Of course we loved it. One of us would have to lie across the narrow ledge at the back covered in a blanket since the front would not seat us all. With Ontario plates we could also play the dumbo Ontarians act if we should be going too fast or had turned right on a red light which was a NONO in Quebec. One picnic at some northern lake stands out. We rented a canoe on arrival but a rainstorm took over and we ended up underneath the overturned boat with our feet sticking out, munching on our soggy sandwiches and laughing heartily. Another time found Bea crouched down in the hospital parking lot trying to tie G.G's fender back on with string. She was spotted by one of the surgeons, also on his way to the hospital, who forthwith joined beauty in distress to make the repairs. And nobody had a camera!!!! In the end Bill won the lottery and he and Bea married. Bill went off to war and only after his return could they settle down and raise a family of four.

    Another classmate, Barb Wells, figured largely in Christmas partying one year. Her doting mother in Saskatchewan had cooked a turkey, packed it with other goodies and mailed it to Barb. Of course we fell upon it like starving Armenians and the treasure was stored under the owner's bed for daily orgies. We are speaking here of nurses learning all about germs and how to avoid falling prey to them! On about morning seven Bea and Hemmie woke up with violent symptoms of food poisoning and staggered off to the infirmary. The greenish remains under the bed succumbed to the garbage can, Happily the rest of us escaped. Whoever heard of a refrigerator in a nurses' residence?

    Epic events often arrive out of the blue and may not even seem that big a deal. Max and I were enjoying our ice cream cones as we

strolled down University Street one sunny summer afternoon when we caught sight of two familiar figures heading our way.  There were Jane Maclean and Dorothy Dunn no less whom we had met over the "floating" bridge games at Western.  A link with home was a rare treat and we felt like drowning sailors who had been tossed a life belt.  It seemed that Dorothy had graduated in French from Catholic Brescia Hall at Western and Jane with a B.A. in business from the Arts College and they had discovered a mutual desire to hone their French language skills by moving in with a French family in Montreal.  Once bilingually fluent they had managed to get jobs in the French sector and were now living in a small one bedroom apartment at the corner of University and Sherbrooke ($32.50 a month rent).  In no time flat their blessedly convenient digs  became the Home away from Home of  the gang now known as the "Four Horsemen".  What bliss it was to hike down the hill of an evening…climb the three flights of stairs (no elevator) and relax over a noggin with our now den mothers.  Time with dark-haired talkative "Dort" and sparky little Jane was full of good talk and laughter and we soon learned to time the exit race up the hill to the last minute.  Dort and Jane were not above a little forgery on notes presumably from visiting relatives to get us extra free hours.  When time came for their vacations back home to St. Thomas we gladly took over the key.
Unfortunately they forgot to tell us that they would be back a day early so we were caught in the midst of a noisy party and a proper cleanup not yet done.  Of course den mothers  always forgive their errant young!   I doubt if we ever properly thanked the saintly pair for adding some sparkle to four often tedious lives.  I owe them  extra halos  since no member of my family was able  to attend my
graduation and they filled the gap like pros.  Those happy 2101 University Street memories will never fade.

A favorite memory of the day we got our caps, 1939, and became (in our minds) official cleaners!

Five years of slavery behind us at last! Graduating at Western 1942.

## 22. THE FINAL CASTLE DAYS

Dear patient readers. If this has become for you a long drawn-out exercise…perhaps that is the point! You are sharing what was interminable to us…and necessary now to fill out the picture. To help us cope we had a calendar and religiously marked off each day…inching away at closing the gap. Our strategy to escape doldrums included jaunts like nipping down to the Berkeley Hotel on Sherbrooke Street to pass an evening over one Old Fashioned (a whole dollar each). Dear Mrs. Chesham knew we would want to sample such a sinful practice and recommended that as pretty harmless. An orgy of "sticky buns" from Pegroid's Bakery often filled the bill. One happy occasion when Bea, Hemmie, Max and I managed a time together was our half-way mark…a big red X on the calendar…duly celebrated in a pub and including a taxi to save the sprint back up the hill. For me the other milestone event was my $21^{st}$ birthday (April 10, 1940)…the end of the Trust Company, the Official Guardian and very close to the end of my dwindling inheritance. That party took place in my room over Pegroid buns and potato salad and stifled laughs and whispers since it was past 10 o'clock "lights out". Hardly hilarious. Of course, once they came on the scene, Jane and Dorothy's digs were a real blessing.

Besides the few jaunts in "Grumble Guts" our outdoor life was pretty sparse. We did occasionally rent bicycles on a day off. Once we rode the length of St Lawrence Main to Point Clair…no mean feat. That day I added to my stiff muscles by sitting in a bed of poison ivy calling for a stint in the infirmary. There actually were a couple of tennis courts behind the hospital and Max and I were part of an R.V.H. team that played a round with our arch enemies at Montreal General…and trounced them. For a walk anytime we enjoyed the winding road up the mountain with parkland to loiter in and lovely views of the city.

Interesting to note that Separatism was a non-issue in Montreal in those days…at least for the large English population. We certainly didn't realize the resentment among the French residents wanting their own language to be used rather than ours. Shops and restaurants, all signs, in fact all businesses, used English. The radio station we tuned in on was in English. When we left after our close-to three years we knew no more French than when we arrived. We had no need to venture into the French parts of the city except as sightseers. Once the war was on it was the Germans who were the bad guys.

I remember Hilda took me to see "Gone With the Wind" at Shea's theatre where the huge organ rose up to the stage, the organist playing rousing tunes.  The movie was so long there was an intermission.  The drinks and popcorn concessions were still not filling the lobby.  Brother Larry was a major in the Queen's Own Rifles and would soon be called up.

For me there was one super "dread" that hung over my head back at R.V.H. and one day when I rushed down to read the duty roster there it was…"Miss Dampier…Operating Room".   My stomach lurched.  We had no official briefing and knew only that we should show up early at one of the two anaesthetic rooms where the student who had set them up last week would clue us in.   The two rooms were at opposite ends of the OR.  I can still hear the raucous shout from Head Nurse Miss Etter as I rushed to cope with one of them, "Why isn't this room set up - get here on the double Miss Dampier!"  Heart pounding I raced to do her bidding - praying I wouldn't also win the anaesthetist's wrath.  I lost 6 pounds those first weeks.  There was no central department for providing the sterilized equipment required in the operating theatres as there is now …mostly pre-packaged - gloves, instruments, trays etc…some items for one use only and then discarded.   In our "spare" time, usually on night duty,  it was our job to wash, dry, powder and wrap the gloves, check the needles and sharpen them if necessary (not skinny and almost painless like now), and set up the complicated trays for various operations.  Everything went into the huge autoclaves to be sterilized under immense pressure.   They were like monsters preparing to explode! (Pressure cookers work by the same principle so I was able to use one of those in my kitchen without blowing the lid off as one friend did, driving the burner right down into the stove!)  Oxygen tanks were still trundled around manually at top speed to the rooms that needed them, and there were often harassed nurses trying desperately to locate one needed no doubt to save a life.  There were no intensive care units or patient rooms provided with every kind of up-to-date equipment as today provides.  One wonders how both patients and their caregivers survived.  They did get good patient care at least.  A postscript to my operating room experience was that I came down with German measles half way through.  This caused a real panic in view of vulnerable surgery patients.  Horrified, I was practically frog-marched to a special "strong" room used for violent patients - bars on the windows and no taps on the bath- tub.  My meals were pushed under the door and I was completely isolated for the number of days required to get rid of that pesky rash.   I was allowed a phone which only allowed me to talk to my friends having a party without me, treating me as their favorite joke!   Those were long boring days.  Released, I had to wash my hair and have a good scrub before re-joining the human race.

A word here about patients' rooms. For one thing no big wards any more. Modern care calls for each room to be equipped for all routine procedures like oxygen, intravenous, blood pressure. No more chasing down the halls. We are now also blessed with whole rooms full of complicated machines...ultra sound...MRI...bone density...and other diagnostic tools. Small wonder that funds are running out. Yet what miracles are being performed. Royal Vic had a reputation for being one of the most up-to-date hospitals in Canada and being accepted to train there was a plum. Actually I paid $25 for the privilege, to be returned if I did no damage. Dropping a whole container of glass thermometers on the floor (now antiques) took care of that. At least they didn't bill me extra! Now R.V.H. is only one among a host of modern facilities. Speaking to older nurses we realized, primitive though it still seemed in our day, just how many advances there had been over the twenty years before. Both world wars spawned exciting new treatments for complicated injuries, plastic and other surgery. At least some good came out of the horrors.

Another area where treatment was dramatically different from now was infections and the spread of diseases. Sulphanilamide (sulpha for short) had just come on the market but the advent of penicillin and other antibiotics was still around the corner. Infectious disease cases were isolated to prevent their spread. In fact we had three months training at the Royal Alexandra Communicable Disease Hospital in Lachine. Each ward treated it's own disease; measles, whooping cough, diphtheria, scarlet fever. Each patient was in a completely enclosed cubicle, which included a sink where the taps were operated by the elbow. We wore short sleeved tops, and when ready to leave a cubicle, had to scrub hands and arms up to the elbow for three minutes. Before long, skin was red and raw and we barely survived the three months without infections ourselves. Everything used by the patient had to be sterilized if possible or exposed to direct sunlight for a prescribed time. If there was any cross infection from one disease to another, the nurses were held responsible and it went on their record. Even simple rules must not be broken. Miraculously the system worked and there were practically no cross infections...none while we were there.

Our ambition during our stay at the communicable disease hospital was to remain unnoticed. Two exceptions I recall. I was hauled out of bed once for piling the laundry improperly in the cupboard...and secondly for admitting a patient without cutting her fingernails. I still can't see how that spread any germs. Good thing they couldn't read my silent lips. Smoking was strictly forbidden at that venue. I horrified even my friends by crawling into our clothes cupboard for a wee puff. How desperate can a girl get? Apart from burning the place down ...had I been caught...?

Most of those diseases are now preventable and that hospital in Lachine is long gone. It's hard to remember the panic that the words diphtheria or scarlet fever could produce. Infections are returning though and hand washing is back as the best way to cope with them.

The last cross was finally added to our calendar. I think it was my popular suggestion to use our scissors and convert our pink and white uniforms into hoola skirts, then dance wildly down the residence halls hugging one another and anyone we met before consigning them (the uniforms!) to the waste baskets. It was stunning to find that a few of out classmates had managed to get married. Discovered they would have been cut off forever. The graduation ceremony happened on a stiflingly hot night when we were done up in our first pure white long-sleeved stiff uniforms, clutching red roses and perspiring mightily. It was a long blur. I was on night duty and true to the times, after getting my diploma I had to hike back to the obstetric ward., hiding my bright red nails. Our foursome had one bonus in that it was impossible for us to work off every day we had missed which was the rule and usually meant every student ended on her own day. We were actually a few days late already getting back to register for our Public Health year at Western so, happily the end came for us together.

## 23. PARTY

And what of that vow we made back on Jan. 31/39, shaking hands on the train taking us to Montreal and vowing to have a big celebration if we all made it? A bonus to help the plan was that we had to be excused any catch-up of time lost. An exact record was kept of sick time for each student and at the end that time had to be made up. That meant classmates didn't finish together but straggled off. But the Four Horsemen all had to leave on the same day in order to get back to London for our final year at Western. Even at that we were a week late for our London registration. It was great fun to at last rent two adjoining rooms at the Mount Royal Hotel and invite one and all to drop in and help us celebrate. First on the agenda was to get the scissors and make hula skirts out of our pink and white striped uniforms...an almost sacrilegious deed After laughing whirls around our rooms they were consigned to the waste basket. All evening, depending on their schedules, friends dropped in to our rooms and then went back up the hill to work. Bill Cameron was in charge of a generous Bar, but we were "drunk on freedom" from beginning to end. We had made it! We had come full circle from that send-off 2 3/4/long years ago. The next morning I remember having to go back to the hospital for some reason and it was such a strange feeling knowing that I no longer belonged - even though we had crossed off the days on our calendar...we couldn't wait to be done with it. Human reactions are strange. One bit of information that stunned us was discovering which of our classmates had somehow managed to get married during their training years! They would have been dismissed had that come to light. I couldn't help admiring their gumption but what a risk they took!

Ah yes...an ending but a new beginning was awaiting us at the end of the coming train ride.

## 24. TEEN TIME

I'm going to sandwich in an earlier period that just can't be neglected. In 1932 my Strathroy buddies and I bid farewell to Public School. Nowadays there are graduation ceremonies complete with gowns and caps even for Kindergarten youngsters...but this was Grade 8...Entrance Class...the all important launching pad for High School. We were given a piece of paper with the evidence. By chance that was also the point at which Mrs. Pugsley decided to decamp from Strathroy and settle us all in London where her girls Connie and Marg could attend Western. Sister Marjorie and brother Larry were already registered and for a period the new two floor apartment on Central Ave. was home for the whole kit and kaboodle of us...not to forget Ted. That was a mingling of strong, often competing personalities that was doomed from the start...a story I will spare my readers. Suffice to say that Marjorie and Larry and later Ted found other accommodations thus solving the problem. Not just the humans suffered from being uprooted. Mrs.P.s handsome tomcat Mickey whom I adored was forthwith given away to a neighbour before we left town with strict instructions to keep him in for a couple of weeks until he got used to his new home. Some time after the deadline time we made a trip back and there was "Billy Big Feet" on the steps to his old digs waiting for us meowing loudly his disapproval.. So into the car he went with joy all round. I always say there is a lot to learn from our felines.

It was just a short walk along Waterloo Street from Central Ave. to Central Collegiate and the first day I practically skipped all the way. I can still see the nice brown and orange wool dress I had invested in for this new venture. The imposing two-storey red brick building loomed into sight. It had an entrance at one end for the girls and one at the other for boys and staff could use the impressive central main door. The halls inside were lined with traditional gray lockers and teemed with students. I was thrilled to locate my very own locker and have the key work and then find where my new home room IE was located. I was not so pleased with sighting an exact replica of my new dress walking by! I'd just have to smile and swallow my pride. At least she wasn't 1E!

Although that building still stands there have been inevitable changes. There was no parking lot. A few cars owned by teachers were parked on the street. I greeted the double tennis courts with joy. I longed to learn to play. Thankfully not until after my time did the courts make way for a parking lot for the influx of wheels. Inside there was no real library…just a few seldom-used shelves in one double classroom. Now there is no doubt a communication centre with computers and printing machines and all the other techie paraphernalia I don't pretend to understand. I believe Day Care has its place which reminds me that in the five years I spent at Central there was only one girl (and in our class) who had to leave because she was pregnant…what a disgrace! One day she did have the courage to bring the stroller over and show off the child. We sensed her sadness when she couldn't join us as we returned to class. She was before her time. Now the statistics at Central are in line with the times. Hence the Day Care. And imagine absolutely no smoking even out on the street and none of the drugs that plague high schools these days. We may have been minus the technology but were also spared the temptations of addictive smoking and drugs.

My greatest trauma from the move was leaving my friends of a lifetime back in Strathroy. In 1E I met my first replacement. Plump Maxine Ward had lately moved from Cochrane up north and had the same need. We lost no time and were soon buddies (and later tennis and badminton pals). Here an explanation of the system is called for. We were randomly put in 1E. By the second and following years our marks would be known and the top ones would forever be in the A's. We made it and we met the rest of our girl gang who joined us. Our group adventures are not part of these stories but the people do pop up, so need a one sentence bio. Kay Liddy…very organized dagheter of the head of the psychology department at Western but a good sense of humour; Phyllis Godwin…lovely daughter of a church family who were so good to me through high school; Miriam Morrow…tiny but bright member of a solid London family; Marie Copeman…cute freckle-faced red head who was also smart enough to graduate at 15 and enter medical school.

Perforce we walked everywhere and it was also a pastime for adventures and gossip. Meandering out to Waterloo Street of a morning I would have it timed to meet up with the above organized Kay who would for sure have all her homework done and would as usual rescue me. In warm weather heading south after school we would end up at the double dip emporium on Dundas Street. For ten cents we could then choose two big flavored dips in a cone. My game then was to make mine last the long trek back to Central Ave. Even now it's drool-making. The cold weather was another story. Bundled up after school we would head across town to the arena to watch our team play hockey. We are speaking here of not getting home until dark mid evening in a starved state. Having no funds there was nothing for it but a little harmless (?) skullduggery. We would split and each on her own slip through the Five and Dime store and while passing the candy counter sneak a handful of samples into a coat pocket. Survival achieved…which makes me sympathetic with that fellow in Les Miz who stole the loaf of bread!

Trading our legs for bikes of a Saturday took some wrangling. We didn't all own wheels so it was up to each person to achieve a loan. We would pack up some kind of lunch even managing hot dogs and the makings of a small fire betimes. A favorite spot was a woods out north west High Park area owned by the Lawson family with whom we had a connection to get permission…a splendid private paradise to picnic in. Once (twice?) somebody produced a 5-cent box of 5 Turret cigarettes With much giggling and coughing we tried puffing away but it failed to grab us. We were young of course but entering the generation that would consider smoking the proper sophisticated thing to do. Not a danger signal to be had.

When the weather nixed biking on Saturday or if there was a movie we just had to see we would use our legs and part with 25 cents at Leowes. There wasn't any popcorn available and we didn't have the money to spare anyway. I loved the musicals…"Ziegfield Follies", "Forty Second Street", "Naughty Marietta", "Rose Marie". Fred Astaire was bliss with his "Top Hat and Tails" and many other movies even though the boring scripts just had to be lived through.

We were spared uniforms but didn't spare ourselves. It was de rigueur to wear a pleated skirt and a white middy with a sailor collar. The middy bottom was neatly folded over and over to the waist and then made snug at the back with huge pins. Brown and white saddle shoes completed the outfit. Hair was short but had to be rolled into "sausages" at night and held in place with bobby pins. For gym there were blousy blue bloomers yet!! Thankfully they met their demise soon after we came to be replaced by proper gym shorts. Max and I did take to the tennis courts and also played badminton and volley ball. I would have liked basketball but glasses were not allowed. I was many years short of contact lenses. We had no outdoor sports field for running or jumping. We enjoyed what we had with no complaints.

Something missing? Right….no boys! I had two strikes against me. Coming to a new place was one and being in that pesky top class didn't make the boys admire us. They were all spoken for anyway by the lassies they already knew. Frustrating at times but we could make up for it later. As a final word here is the Central song without the tune:

> *In this good old Forest City where we love to dwell,*
> *Where the girls are always pretty and the boys are swell,*
> *If you want to pick a winner, though the stakes are high,*
> *You will find the very best are in the C.C.I……*

*In the C.C.I....C.C.I...gold and purple colours
we will wear and proudly cry
For the C.C.I....C.C.I...we will shout until we die
FOR THE C.C.I............!*

Back to the real world that greeted the end of the teens.

## 25. THE AFTER SHOCK

There was to be no gradual changeover for the recently liberated nursing foursome...but first we had to settle in.  The London-bound train dropped us into the arms of welcoming families.  My sister and I and my luggage headed for the Pi Beta Phi sorority house on Waterloo Street where I had reserved a spot to bed down.  Not that I was at all in favour of sororities.  I resented that the headquarters being in the States meant money was being held, to be sent there after the war.  Besides I felt that questionable criteria were used in selecting "desirable" recruits.  However there were still no student residences so this was my best bet.  Pi Phi had a large attractive house, well run by a pleasantly efficient house mother and the price was right ($35 per month...meals included).  Problem number one met me immediately...despite my reservation every bed was already occupied.  The answer to my plight was a bed out on an unheated veranda.  A cold autumn spell had me huddling under a pile of blankets and hi-tailing it inside in the morning through my own frosty breath.

I only heard the comment later but apparently we returnees were looked upon by our fellow students with awe as mature adults with real life experiences.  By the same token the bevy of fresh-faced pretty young things looked more like high-schoolers to us.  Conversation leaned heavily toward the latest date (hunk?)...the next party...what outfit to wear. It didn't take long though for us to relax our "mature" role and blend happily into co-ed life once again.. Very soon there was a vacancy for me on the top layer of a bunk bed...but absolutely an impasse as far as squeezing any of my clothing onto the jammed cupboard rod.  Cute black-haired Mitsy simply smiled sweetly as she proudly freed up a few inches.  Soon it all became fun even as we realized that clouds were gathering.  This was late September of 1941 after all and already the war was taking many eager young male scholars.  Rationing was part of life which still seemed much as usual.  Partings and losses lay ahead.

The immediate after shock for us was that we had not as yet written our Registered Nursing exams.  Because we had trained in Quebec we had to use their version and the papers had duly been sent on ahead to the Institute of Public Health.  That sombre three-storey gray brick building was away down in South London on the corner of the Victoria Hospital Property...a good long hike I soon learned.  We were no longer to be part of the lovely rolling green north campus.  Tall stern

Dr. Slack was in charge and in our first two days we wrote the twelve RN papers!!! They tended to the practical perforce but it was still an exhausting exercise. It took a few weeks to learn we had all passed and get the precious documents. Fortunately I had a scholarship to pay the $120 tuition fee...an unbelievable bargain by today's standards. My journalism bent also won me second place in the province of Quebec which I only mention because of an amusing twist. The girl who came first was also an RVH grad who shortly thereafter had a mental breakdown. I took a lot of ribbing as friends avoided me in case I exploded!!!

Hemmie's mother "Mardo" helped us enjoy our free time. Baker Street was handy to the school but we had been told that lunch would not necessarily be provided. One day we decided to ignore the ban but as we turned in to the front door we saw Mrs. C. peering out the living room window. By the time we were inside she was stretched out on the floor with eyes rolled back! Of course she forgave and fed us. At other times she would play the piano as we danced and pranced about...a release after a morning of learning about "potable" water and properly-built septic systems from stern Dr.Slack. I joined the after dinner bridge games with gusto at the Sorority House and soon made friends. Best of all I finally had a better room on the third floor to myself...my neighbors soon complaining loudly about my snoring.

We didn't realize that the photograph of four smiling, capped and gowned graduates taken on a sunny June day in 1942 was also a farewell to the close-knit group that had formed on the same site in September 1937. This time our class led the procession from Little stadium up to the Arts building where our families had gathered for this final happy ritual. Meantime, with a lingering nostalgia we had all applied for summer jobs with the VON (Victorian Order of Nurses) in Montreal. It turned out they only wanted one and it was me...just by a draw since the applications were exactly alike. I accepted. Not long after, Bea married her Bill Cameron and he went off overseas while she worked at Public Health. I was stunned to find that Hemmie had joined the armed forces and was slated for overseas on hospital duty immediately. I should have known. It was a military family her father being a colonel in World War1 and her brother a major in the present one. Hemmie advanced later to Matron status. Max would have liked to go too but due to having only one functioning eye was not accepted so she opted for school nursing. The Powers that Be had actually begged us to stay since the loss of so many nurses was leaving the home front short.

Clutching my remaining $50 inheritance and my suitcase I took off for 2101 University Street in July having talked Jane and Dorothy into having a boarder. The dears welcomed me but I would have to sleep on the couch which was fine with me. Memories of that summer point to some outdated conditions. I don't think the temperature ever dropped below 90'F.  Each day, clutching my list from the office I set off for the Jewish area around St. Lawrence Main completely garbed in my navy wool suit, black hose, oxfords and felt hat...lugging a leather work satchel...no consideration for temperature.   No cars in use by VON in those days so it was "shanks mare", or streetcar.  One small plus...there was still respect for uniforms in those days and my outfit generally at least got me a seat on the crowded streetcars.   Nowadays VONs are as casually and comfortably dressed as school kids on vacation and unrecognizable as to their calling.   And they drive cars!   After work I staggered up the three flights of stairs at 2101 where Jane and Dorothy made way as I headed for the shower, shedding as I went, before facing the evening meal.  Did we have air conditioning?   You have to be kidding!

There was satisfaction to be had, especially starting the day with Moms and their newborns fresh from the hospital.  The wails of woe could be heard before the door was opened by the fraught mother.  Little more than a ½ hour later the baby was cooing (Fed? Burped? Rash soothed?).  Baby equipment had been retrieved from all over the house and stowed handily.  Peace reigned.  Nurse had a friend for life.  In the afternoon the patients were for sure at the opposite end of life...aging, usually chronically ill and in need of firm but gentle care with family caregivers no less grateful.   On another level...assisting doctors with home births wasn't allowed without a learning session and familiarity with the secrets of the "birthing" suitcase.  The staff person who called me in the middle of one night soon after I arrived and said I had to go on my own to a given address bag in hand would not listen to my pleas of complete ignorance.  Just "You are it...now GO!"   And she hung up. Forthwith the suitcase and I, trembling, were delivered to the said address and the doctor arrived just in time to see the baby sliding into my shaking hands.  I failed to see why he found my aghast expression and staring eyes so amusing.  The night staff girl was forthwith disciplined and I was sent home to recover in the hands of my admiring room-mates!

Having a mainly Jewish clientele in my area made for a unique twist.   Our Saturday was their Sabbath, a day with many rules to be "religiously" followed.   There was to be no cooking or any other work done in my clients' homes which required ingenuity on their part.  They could not light the stove or do several other household chores but the nurse could easily fill in for them.  The saving angel was greeted with beaming faces and extra treats on the Sabbath.

Overall though I wasn't really ready to settle into such a restricted lifestyle yet.  Little did I know that the genie in the bottle might come to the rescue.  Of course...that has to wait for the next entry!

## 26. THE GENIE POINTS NORTH

My genie was in the form of a letter which arrived at 2101 at the end of that hot summer of '42. The sender was Fran Powell...chief industrial nurse at Ontario Hydro in Toronto. Fran had graduated a year ahead of us and I knew her only slightly. The letter informed me that there was a position available for a nurse at the Abitibi Canyon settlement and if I would like to apply my fare to and from Toronto for an interview would be taken care of. Tired at the end of another hot work day and never having heard of the place I promptly poo-pooed the idea. Dear Jane and Dorothy exchanged a glance. "You don't care to enjoy a free return trip to Toronto...never mind the job?" asked Dorothy. Hmm...free trip...friends to visit...no need to accept the job? I did an about turn and in no time my answering note accepting the offer was on its way. I was soon aboard the trusty CNR...pre VIA Rail... for TO. Fran filled in the gaps. A large Hydro plant spanned the Abitibi River a few miles south of Moosonee on the southern tip of James Bay. The T&NO Railway (Tamiskaming and Northern Ontario) serviced the gap from Cochrane north. Does this ring some bells? Remember our new housekeeper Mrs. H. and her daughter Daisy back in 1923 boarding the ship at Moosonee to sail north and down around Labrador to the St. Lawrence in order to reach the westbound train for Strathroy? My genie was responsible for a strange coincidence, having me "ride the rails" that had been laid too late for them. Yes...the more I learned the more this adventure became irresistible. I signed on the dotted line and agreed to plan my arrival at the Canyon for January 1, 1943.

Back in Montreal I had a major bullet to bite. I had only recently been promoted to a full time position in the VON. Miss Moag, Old School Disciplinarian Personified, was aghast. I quote (it was burned into my memory), " Miss Dampier...you will soon be unacceptable professionally without daily supervision from your betters". On the contrary, that sounded mighty acceptable to me!

Here is a thumbnail sketch of my new destination. It was as though the Hydro settlement had been dropped complete into the barren bush three miles in from the T&NO rail line making necessary a connecting spur line into the Canyon. Thirty five two-storey employee frame homes circled a large barren area served by a road which faced all the back doors. Front doors went unused. At one end of the road stood the two-room schoolhouse where two teachers taught grades 1 through 13. Close by the store run by Vince Maisonneuve carried necessary food and housekeeping needs as well as having the Post Office in the hands of postmistress Dot Frampton. Unlike today no one else under any circumstances was allowed into her domain for which she had been licensed. At the other end of the road was the cottage hospital with a neat apartment on one side furnished in maple for the nurse and an office and patient bedroom on the other. Nearby a Staff House for the single workers included the dining room where the nurse also ate her meals. An arena and a recreation building completed the layout. There was a small settlement for the native workers and families further into the bush.

Fran warned me that the arrival of a new nurse was an epic event in the Canyon so I must be prepared for a hearty welcome. I was sad to leave Dorothy and Jane who had made me so welcome and seen me through my Montreal challenges. With hugs all round I headed for TO and then north to Cochrane in time to connect to the 10 a.m. T&NO train on January 1. Winter blanketed the town as I followed others crossing the tracks to the local hotel on a main street of nondescript stores. Coffee having been scoffed I noted the time and headed for my train only to be told that the timetable was a myth. The train would go when the engineer darn well got around to it. Seems he often stopped in the season to get off and pick a batch of berries or milk the cow. Much later I was even aboard when we wheeled into a siding and watched the engine take off with the crew for a lumber camp and a few hours of dinner and relaxation while we fumed. Hence T&NO really meant Time No Object!. Also on this first trip no one thought to mention that I'd better buy some food in Cochrane as there would be none available on the train…so I starved!

The station where the spur line started was Fraserdale which we eventually reached late afternoon while the train continued on to Moosonee. The Hydro jitney…a cute two coach number forthwith met its only passenger and we rumbled through the wintry bush to the Canyon. I took a deep breath and climbed to the platform. Not a soul in sight…at least except for a rather dull young lady who had apparently been given the welcoming stint and managed to direct me and my luggage to my cottage before taking off. A good hot meal in the Staff House soothed my bruised ego. The next morning stooping arthritic plant manager Mr. Fergusin finally appeared with warm apologies. It seemed that the whole colony was sleeping off two solid weeks of Christmas/New Years festivites! I was good and never recounted that non-welcome to Fran!

## 27. LIFE IN THE CANYON?

In many ways this was an ideal living setup. Houses were supplied and not surprisingly heated with Hydro. However the furnaces were built to use hardwood which was available for those with the energy to help themselves and build a woodpile in their yard. I noted that no matter how efficiently the heat was produced there was always a rim of ice around the base of the rooms all winter. Minus 50 ' Fahrenheit was the lowest I experienced when I was cautioned not to run or I could nip my lungs. Skiing was made possible by a wide swath having been cut through the bush during the fall to make winding trails and even mini hills to scoot down. We just kept our skis stuck in a drift outside our doors. Felt boots were de rigueur for warmth. We also wore them in the indoor rink where we could slide around playing broomball. Indoor also was a badminton court and the space was great for the dances every other Saturday night. The in between ones provided a movie which had an intermission every time a reel had to be rewound. Entertainment always readily available.

In Summertime the weather was beautiful…warm and sunny and completely frustrating. Unknowingly I set out to visit someone with freshly-washed hair and in no time was rushing back with blood streaming down my neck. Blackflies came and plagued us all through the season outlawing sleeveless dresses or uncovered heads or lawn chairs. In the evening the flies passed the feast over to the mosquitoes who swarmed in for their share…in spite of which we covered ourselves with goo and lit smudge pots and played tennis as late as 10 p.m. in the long northern evenings. The "flies in the ointment" didn't stop the fun.

On a personal level I found kindred spirits for bridge games. Saturday nights after the movie or dance our foursome would gather and proceed to spend the rest of the night dealing out the cards using our own set of rules. One of my extras was the church service the next morning. Once a month a Church Army member came in to officiate. The other weeks I filled in with a service from the Book of Common Prayer while another recruit played the pump organ for a goodly number of attendees.
No sermon I promise you! I must have fallen into bed for the rest of the day hoping for no crisis calls.

There were special treats. It became routine to gather at my digs of an evening when our order of a quart of whipping cream had come in on the train. This would be dumped in the hand-cranked ice cream machine along with bananas…strawberry jam….whatever. Then we would just beat it into submission and fill big bowls for a late night snack. Lacking that we would buy a great slab of cheese from Vince and make grilled cheese sandwiches by the stack in my kitchen. It amounted to meal #4 for me who never gave up breakfast as the others did. In summer too the avid fishermen would ignore the mosquitoes and go out for a catch. If they returned with a big pickerel the word would go out and the orgy would be fresh fried fillets at the staff house. While we are on food I soon learned a trick at the meals. A large platter full of the meat for that dinner was at centre table. The trick if you wanted a good helping was to grab a fork on the way in and stab a piece on the way by. Otherwise you might be an unintended vegan! No wonder it took me five years to get rid of the results of all those calories.

    Those memories are still so clear to me and there are more good ones to come…but a breather is called for. Time for a "feetsup" in the easy chair.

## 28. THE GENIE FINISHES THE JOB

It wasn't all beer and skittles for the nurse at the Canyon believe me. Just being on call 24 hours a day and having a train only twice a week was stressful. When needed if I was not reached by phone two blasts on the blower outside would bring me running. What a boon a cell phone would have been...to say nothing of E-Mails and I-Pads and the dozens of apps I never will figure out. Life was calm mostly but the fear of an epidemic of some kind always threatened. One woman was a special thorn in my flesh and liked to call me early in the morning to make sure I was up and at it. Once one of her several children developed swollen glands which she was sure was mumps. I was as certain it was not. So we waited through the several weeks incubation period with my fingers permanently crossed and my nerves jumpy. No other cases developed so I had won that round. One of my duties was to inoculate the children for the few diseases then thus prevented. One mother and child were walking ahead of me one day and I heard Mom say to her sprite..."You be good or I'll take you to the nurse and she'll stick you with a needle"! This inoculation service was shared with a contingent from Iroquois Falls further south on the rail line. One train of the weekly two only came as far as us and then went back. That meant the group of youngsters and parents from the Falls could come to Fraserdale Station to meet me. With my kit in hand I would ride out on our spur and do the job. The engineer agreed to wait to take them back. The mothers were grateful and it provided a pleasant little social time on the station benches for us while the young ran wild. That worked well until the day that I forgot the vital needles. I had to be run back to get them and the engineer was barely civil about the extra delay. On the T&NO I wonder what difference an extra hour would make? There were other routine public health chores like examining the students regularly for any obvious problems. There was a real need for tooth care especially among the native children. A dentist did make trips in every few months and set up his business in my medical room using a dental chair stored in one corner. Coaxing the youngsters to visit him was the hard part.

Our aboriginal families preferred to use their own native medicines but did occasionally ask for the nurse to visit. Going into their tents (which they could just move instead of using and caring for their company houses) when they were trying to kill a batch of germs with piles of blankets and heat was to get a steam bath yourself. These fellow citizens found it difficult to change from their old ways of life and accept ours.  That problem has yet to be solved.

A few other crises made my presence worthwhile.

…How about the day I answered my door to see a man wearing a fedora hat with blood pouring down from under it on all sides.  It seems he had warned his men to stay out of the way of the crane but neglected to do it himself.  It was actually a small scalp wound.  And you are right…no obligatory hard hats for workers then.

…The women were supposed to head out for Cochrane to have their young.  They disliked the waiting away from home so left the exit as late as possible.  I sat in my finery all through a New Year's Eve party while one little creature threatened to come along early…but happily didn't.  The party people kept dropping in to check on our progress.  One other new arrival wouldn't hold off and since the fellow nurse I hoped to recruit as helper begged off I handled that one alone.  Relief all round when all went well!  The little girl was forthwith named Mary.

…Another critical time was when a new male employee developed violent abdominal pains and we had to use the motorized rail work "jigger" to take the two of us on a bouncing chilly trip on the rails to the Cochrane hospital.  Unfortunately he did not survive.  We learned that the army had discharged him with an inflamed appendix undiagnosed and in the wrong spot.

…Perhaps my most difficult episode was when a young female employee did an unexpected twist down a ski hill, causing a serious leg fracture.  We managed to splint it and she lay in pain in the hospital bed while the men searched for a bush pilot to take her out.  Unbelievably I had no morphine to ease the pain.  After a sleepless night for both of us a pilot having a haircut in Timmins flew in and loaded us on for the trip out.  I prayed while the pilot tried to find a field large enough for the plane to land without crashing into a fence.  After a couple of unsuccessful swoops we managed to coast to within inches of a post.  Those pilots were an incredible lot of fearless fellows as I found on several occasions.

…A frantic call one day brought me on the double to a woman whose face was puffed up almost out of recognition.  She had unknowingly eaten a sandwich containing shrimp to which she was dangerously allergic.  Fortunately I had adrenalin to bring her back to normal.

…Dear  Mr. Ferguson the superintendent had severe arthritis. He put wool over his hands on an ironing board every morning and used a warm iron to get his fingers able to write.  His doctor had sent in a series of gold injections to be administered by the nurse into his chest muscles over a period of time.  Question…Should I tell him  I had never learned how to do such a procedure and let him suffer or pray and give it a try? The prayer was answered and the treatment was successful.

On my arrival the colony had appeared to be all flat land. It wasn't until the deep snow had melted away that the attractive contours of low walls and slopes and valleys became visible. Some of that snow would stay buried in protected spots ready for the ice cream maker as late as June. The most stunning visual treats came during the winter. One I remember was after a surface thaw and then freeze when at night the whole snow-covered landscape sparkled in the moonlight and the smoke drifting lazily from the chimneys made a fairyland. Not to forget the galaxy of colours of the aurora borealis when it chose to roll and dance across the night skies.

There is one event that I can still chuckle over. For background...the nurse could expect to be the subject of teasing at the hands of the single men employees. For instance I had to let the office know where I was at all times...but how about having a bath? A dangerous announcement. I had to settle for a "slam dunk" system. At one point I came home to find my tormenters had switched the furniture in my apartment between bedroom and living room just for the laughs.. Turning the tables happened by chance. You may remember meeting Bea, our femme fatale in our nursing foursome. Well...I decided to invite her for a few days stay in my northern retreat. Off the train she came and enjoyed her first evening meal in the staff dining room. The next day I was stunned and could hardly stifle my laughter. That rather scruffy, tousled, untidy lot had gone through a metamorphosis. Clean, neat, spit and polish was the name of the game. All to no avail. Bea had been there before and could not be pried from my side while they moped. I loved it. Bea entered into the spirit of the place though...skiing, broomball, badminton. I guess I didn't realize what good shape I was in. Apparently her family were not impressed when she hobbled off the train with a crick in her neck from the hard hospital mattress and a host of aching joints.

Did the Canyon have any war effects? The only one I experienced was rationing. Dot Frampton next door was suffering withdrawal symptoms from lack of her favorite Chelsea buns. One night she rebelled and proceeded to use every last bit of her butter and sugar ration to make a pan of them. I sat through the whole mix, roll and "slather" of the sugary goo...and then the baking. It was bedtime by the time we piled into them savoring every gooey mouthful. We did save some for her boys but only because any more would have been disastrous.

The "nothing is perfect" factor applied even to Abitibi Canyon. After a couple of years I could see why most of the men had an application at Head Office requesting a transfer. I too began to feel a need to connect with my friends and colleagues in the outside world.

Just the same my experiences there had filled a gap in my professional life.  A large hospital like Royal Vic gave no space to its nurses to handle responsibility on their own.  Doctors and Head Nurses were always on hand to bear the burden.  The Canyon gladly dumped it all into my lap.  Technically I still had to contact the doctor in Cochrane by phone and get his OK for anything I did.  It was soon obvious that for every combination of symptoms he would have the same answer…so I was really diagnosing the problems myself.  It may have been a chancy method but it was also exhilarating and fortunately didn't ever let me down…a real learning experience.  After two years though I notified Head Office that I would  be heading south  again, presumably to look for a job.  By a stroke of luck (and the war) they were able to offer me a transfer to Head Office instead which I happily accepted.

   In contrast to my Non-Welcoming arrival my sendoff was a Regretful-Warm gathering.  Two small incidents stay with me.  Being wartime I had scarcely tasted my favorite bananas.  The jolly plump cook's farewell gesture was a banana cream pie and my last day I ate every crumb of it myself.  The other I learned later.  My cute little male pussycat up and had a litter of kittens!  So much for my knowledge of anatomy.

   Progress  has again  altered the Canyon  and its approaches.  I believe the T&NO rail line has been replaced by roads and the plant itself is operated by technology leaving the settlement deserted.  I'm left with my mental pictures and these stories to trigger a host of great memories.

## 29. OUT FRONT IN WARTIME

Leaving the Canyon meant "Going out Front" in their lingo. I thought of it as going back home but soon discovered how unfamiliar city life had become as a result of the war just winding down in 1944. We had had our ears glued to the radio at the Canyon as the long-awaited D-Day invasion was acted out…little realizing how much more foot-slogging and bloodshed was ahead for our troops before the end came.

I still had my father's old expandable "valise" when I boarded the familiar rather rattle-trap southbound passenger car of my friend the T&NO. ..better at least than the ones we had travelled in on the Toronto Montreal run that had been converted to benches for the troops. On this line the natives preferred to stay together in a car of their own. As we sped along I watched longingly for something I had missed up north…a spreading maple tree. The bush abounded with stunted firs that did not sport an eye-catching array of lovely autumn colours. Transferring at Cochrane to the CNR, the landscape gradually changed to rolling farms and villages, finally depositing me at Toronto's Union Station. There I was confronted with noisy bustling crowds with pale strained faces so unlike my easy-going laid-back friends up north. To say nothing of missing breathing the clean brisk northern air. That nostalgia would soon fade.

The impact of the war on living accommodation soon confronted me. By a happy coincidence Jane and Dorothy had decided to make the move from Montreal to Toronto and I gladly offered to find digs for us together. From a temporary boarding arrangement I set out to find an apartment suitable for three professional women. Dreamer! I pounded the sidewalks from one apartment building to another…from waiting lists of only one hundred to those with three hundred. Wartime had brought building to a standstill. My desperation finally landed us a large upstairs room that would hold our three cot-sized day beds, in a big red brick home in the Bathurst St Clair area. The outside was actually quite attractive but inside was a warren of about 20 rooms right up to the attic with two bathrooms and one kitchen serving all.

If I were aiming to write a pot boiler novel all that went on behind those resident closed doors would provide the plot. For Memoirs best to leave them unopened. The owner of this domain was a busybody by the name of Miss Peden whose pursed lips matched her name. Her favorite pastime was posting notes such as "Do not put a small pot on a large burner" or "please keep to your own section of the refrigerator". The one that gave us the best chuckle was "DO NOT REMOVE MY NOTES!"

We found that she spent a good deal of her time wasting our rent at the races. Each room had one foot-wide section of cupboard and counter in the kitchen. How we managed to cook quite respectable meals and then carry them up to our room on a tray to be set out on a card table is now a mystery. We even entertained the occasional friend and found a fourth for bridge in Dorothy's brother Joe. Most astonishing was that on our only day off (Saturday morning was a work day back then and the afternoon for shopping and cleaning) all three of us set forth in Sunday finery to walk to nearby churches. There was a bit of rivalry at work here since the two Anglicans (Jane and I) were not about to be put to shame by faithful Catholic Dorothy. Invariably when we returned there were bathrobe-clad roomers at the kitchen table munching on jam spread toast or in one case eating something unknown from a can!

One memorable day in those few years was in the winter of 1944. I normally took the streetcar to work at Hydro on University Avenue. That morning I opened the door to be met by a wall of snow a good 30 inches high. We soon learned that the city was blanketed and traffic at a standstill. I donned my trusty skis after a tunnel had been cleared and had a glorious run down Bathurst Street bereft of any trams or cars. It was a long hike only to find…hardly surprisingly…that the office was closed. My call to duty ended with a slow uphill return journey in a crammed streetcar. That storm was an epic memory for all Torontonians.

Our battle for living quarters next landed us on the second floor of a semi-detached house where we had our own ice box requiring delivery of huge chunks every other day. The so-called kitchen also had a one burner stove with a tiny oven that could sit on it. That's where we developed the habit of eating at the little table by candlelight to hide our questionable surroundings. The only source of water was the bathroom, shared with our owners downstairs. One large and one small room completed the setup for which they charged by the room at an unconscionable rate. The War bred greed, One advantage was that we were only a couple of blocks from my brother Larry and his family when he returned from his five years of war. It was close to the end of the forties before we achieved our original goal of a bona fide apartment with a real kitchen and a door through which no one could come without our permission. Privacy at last! It might need a complete paint job (what didn't after five neglected years?) but we loved every tacky inch of it. It was not until then that we were unashamed to invite family and friends to share our presentable home.

As well as living with the effects of the war life did go on through various changes, only one of which rates a chapter here. It began as a routine nursing duty ...doling out aspirin and liquids to ailing staff members. This one happened to be tall, male, handsome, and somebody I had been eying for some time. The visit was repeated several times and then one fine day the patient...Ron Mathieson by name...stopped me in the hall and suggested it was time he repaid all those beverages. The die was cast and a date made. I had just recently moved from living for awhile with my brother in his fine home on Oriole Parkway to that humble flat in the two-storey house. Why not have Ron pick me up there? I resisted and it would have been a wasted effort since he was a constant visitor for the next three years before we tied the knot.

The wedding speaks to those times. Having no parents I undertook to arrange the affair myself...that is until Ron, the PR expert, firmly took over my folder. On May 5, 1951 the service would be at Christ Church Deer Park but the venue for the reception the now long gone Kensington Hotel handily next door to the Hydro building. 150 guests were invited, my sister was my Matron of Honour and brother Larry would give me away. Sit down dinners were not yet the style so the guests moved around and socialized at will, being served delicious party hors d'oeuvres and champagne for the toasts. Ron's mother being teetotal and a force in our lives there was no bar. My young nieces and nephews kept it from being a stodgy affair by scooting about and all went swimmingly. The hotel provided a change room for me and the young made good use of their confetti as we left. Why the details? The receipt has disappeared but I paid all of $250 for the complete shebang! I can't believe it myself.

The launching of our trip to New York also rates a telling. To spare his car getting all messed up with confetti Ron stashed it away and used his mother's instead. We felt pretty smug as we drove off in a pristine vehicle. Ron being a friendly type had not been able to resist an invitation to drop in on a party at his friend Tooner Howard's place in Thorold on our way to Niagara. Having put up with all the jokes there we set out at midnight for the hotel and...yes...ran out of gas! Ron had filled up his mother's tank but forgotten his own. After a fraught silence he came up with a plan. I would go into the hotel by way of the next vehicle that came by (A NoNo in 2013). I would ask the hotel to direct me to some gas and send it out to Ron and I would retire. A farmer shortly stopped his Ford and I climbed in among the seed onions in the back seat...finery and all. At the hotel's direction I made my way with many qualms down a dark alley to a scruffy man who spoke no English. He managed to figure out that I needed a can of gas but I would have to go with him. So...off we drove through the pitch dark to the spot...but no Ron...then up and down roads in case I was wrong. I was tempted just to head back to Toronto but eventually in the small hours I was dropped at the hotel where I found Ron having a quaff in our suite as he made up the headline in the Globe for the next morning. "Careless groom loses bride on the Queen Elizabeth!" It seems the RCMP had driven by and told him no gas would be available so they escorted him to Niagara. The atmosphere was a little tricky for awhile but after all it was a happy ending. Eventually that became our favorite Mutt and Jeff party act!

With the war over a whole new era was in the wings waiting to speed up change in a host of areas. Like it or not we are still a part of it.

Going out Front", as it was called, was both exciting and traumatic. I hadn't realized how much I had absorbed the spirit of the north. There were so many people down here, mostly rushing along the crowded streets, looking gray and haggard as compared with my "laid back" northern friends. The air lacked that exhilarating clean crispness that I was used to. Up there I had known everybody...Toronto was full of strangers who didn't know me or care! As I recounted earlier, accommodation was my first priority.

Friend Bea leaning out of the Hydro "Jitney" that brought her in from the main train, 1943.

## 30. A REPEAT OF FAMILY HISTORY

My readers will remember that, back in the Twenties, brave Dad, just turned seventy, invested in that recent invention a Chev touring automobile. In 1947 I had cause to admire his courage as I myself faced taming a more modern version of a Chev vehicle.

One responsibility of the Head Office nurse was to visit employees who were on the sick list. There was a lurking suspicion that an element of policing was part of this service. At the same time I was able to be of help to those who were legitimate. Hydro had several vehicles for the use of management and chauffeurs to drive them and I had also been granted that special privilege. Charlie my driver assured me too that it was accepted policy to slip any little extra personal trips in but I was careful to stay clear of that land mine.

One day, our pleasant Medical Director Dr. Urquhart called me into his office to explain that the Powers That Be had decided this was too expensive a system and they would prefer if I drove myself. "Do you have a driver's license?" he asked. Fingers crossed I fibbed "Oh YES" and I was told that the firm would help me to invest in the necessary vehicle. Thanking my good boss I beat a hasty retreat to the phone book and made an appointment to take a driver's course. Their office was right at Bay and College, a daunting area to launch a driving career. Eight lessons were involved to ready me for my all important test.

The next move was to acquire my wheels and I had the fun of choosing a natty little deep red Chevrolet "business" coupe. This model had a shelf across the back instead of a seat...presumably for briefcases and the like. No seat belts of course. I produced the required $2025 and the deal was done (What an antique treasure that would be in 2013!). The lessons were worse than I had even imagined and for the first few sessions I was a basket case. I would just totter up the stairs (this was the era of the upstairs rooms in a semi-detached house) and fall into bed each night. Thinking of Dad I quieted my churning stomach and persevered...even managing to pass the test. My claim to fame was that my teacher had never before had anyone who could back up better than they could go forward! By now it was September and my car would be ready in a couple of months. I suggested to my new beau that perhaps I could practice a bit on his wheels but Ron shuddered and vetoed any such high risk plan.

It was an icy snow-covered day in January when I got the call to come and pick up my car. It is unbelievable that I managed to steer out into home-going traffic and head up the Avenue Road hill for home. How I managed not to stall my gear shift motor and end my driving career right on the spot I'll never know. I had no garage of course so parked on the street. Early the next morning I climbed into the frigid vehicle for my drive to work without a clue when the cold motor refused to budge. My frustration and that awful grinding noise was noted by a passing milk truck driver who stopped and peering in asked, "Lady…did you ever hear of a thing called a choke?" "As a matter of fact, No, " I replied and had a lesson in Canadian winter driving. By this time Dr. Urquhart was aware of my deceit about a license and it was with a sigh of relief he and the office staff greeted me when I arrived safely each day but generally frazzled and late. There were unwelcome adventures such as backing one wheel over a curb when I had managed to get a garage… professional help being required to heave it back over. Then one day I locked the keys in the car and had to track down Ron to get my second set which I had neglected to put in an accessible place. Happily I did avoid any accidents since it took some skill to drive and at the same time locate street numbers.

As an example of the relaxed rules of the road in the '40's…I undertook to show off to my oldest friend Clara Thomas and drive her to Oshawa to visit friend Ruth Longmire in hospital. Baby John Thomas, only months old, came along for the ride. A blanket was spread on that back shelf and he had a nice amount of space for crawling if he so chose. Not only was he not strapped down but we didn't have seat belts either. I recall it was a pleasant worry free trip! I did involve Dad in my driving by pretending that he had floated down into the seat beside me and was stunned not only by the dials and buttons on the car but the streams of traffic in both directions in the many lanes of 401 highway. It often provided me with an amusing pastime.

I still wince having to cope with a life without wheels. Memories don't make for a very long drive!

Mickey lords it on top of car having won his wish to move to London! 1932.

## 31. NORTH AGAIN...EAR FALLS

Ontario Hydro's ability to drop power plants into the northern wilderness (at least it looked like that) allowed the nurse to make further northern treks.  Having returned from the Canyon in 1944 I was just settling in at Head Office when there came another "call of the wild". This one couldn't have been more different.

The name of the colony was Ear Falls...a small settlement sitting at the top end of Lac Seul, a lake in Northwestern Ontario just 60 miles across as the crow flies but boasting  5000 miles of meandering shoreline.  At the bottom tip was Sioux Lookout...a stop on the CNR line travelling along above Lake Superior.

The cleared area of the settlement held about ten company houses, a community hall, a one-room school and a boarding house providing room and board for the strays such as me and the female teacher.  An unusual touch was a little freezer building for general use...but especially for the hunters and fishermen...the whole place making Abitibi Canyon look like a metropolis. Keeping guard from their outdoor kennels , the sled dogs often filled the night air with their spine-tingling howls.  Best to give them a wide berth.  A snowmobile stretched out to accommodate a few passengers was parked handily nearby.  Not far off in the bush was the usual gathering of native dwellings along with the General Store.  Isolation here was more complete than at Abitibi since besides lacking a road there was also no rail line. Traffic in and out was strictly by bush plane from Sioux Lookout.  Hereby was the catch. Twice during the year even the planes couldn't make it.  In the Spring the ice became too insecure for planes to land and the water not yet open enough for pontoons.  This was "Breakup" time and could last 4 to 6 weeks.  In the Fall the reverse problems arose as the water began to freeze over...but the ice took weeks to become sufficiently solid..."Freezeup" time.  The favorite pastime for the men during both those seasons was measuring the thickness of the ice daily in various spots and keeping the women informed.

Feisty Bill Dowds was the plant manager guaranteeing I soon learned that there would be  excitement stirred up in the life of Ear Falls. It was Bill who had decided that his flock needed the nurse to look after them in the Breakup/Freezeup times.  Apparently I was the first recruit and it was at Breakup.in '44.  With no ground rules I had to make it up as I went along including what the heck to wear and how much to take and what to do when I got there.  One hefty suitcase had to do to be lugged aboard the westbound train.  The stop in Sioux Lookout was in the middle of the night so I was helped up the ladder, suitcase and all, into a top berth, to be wakened and hefted down at one a.m. Why on earth had they not found me a bottom bed at least?

  Sioux Lookout was not a hub of tourism at best but at that hour it was eerie in the dark to follow the poor soul who met me to my boarding house and hope to catch some more shuteye before my morning date for the flight over Lac Seul. All the same it was exciting on a pleasant Spring morning, arrayed in sensible oxfords, my Spring coat and a hat with a daisy for decoration, to climb into the front of the neat little plane along with the pilot. Thrilling too for my first flight ever to fly over the miles of choppy water and to land neatly an hour or so later in what looked like barren wilderness. Here we were met by a dapper little Englishman, Ron Nicholls. He sported a black beret on his head, wellies on his feet and a warm parka in between, and was dead pan at my inappropriate outfit. Playing follow the leader I froze as I sloshed an unexpected two miles over a broad expanse of ankle deep water covering the remainder of the winter landing ice. Ron told me later that he had a hard time controlling his hoots of laughter as my jaunty daisy bobbed in the wind. We travelled the last lap in a boat that took us to Ear Falls, dry land and the boarding house where I could dry off and recover. Here are some of the unique highlights of my several trips to Ear Falls:

  …Bill Dowd's wife Dorothy and their little tots Doreen and Donny were also in residence. The isolation had one plus in that there was no rationing and my weeks were filled with a surfeit of cakes, pies and other sweet goodies from the kitchens of Dorothy and the other super cooks. There were eight or ten youngsters all told and I repeated my unpopular needle inoculation exercises…as usual not endearing me with them. As I remember I also had a popular and sometimes hilarious weekly class in Home Nursing for the mothers to practice caring for one another.

  …Exercise took the form of walks…more like sloshing as we struggled through the melting bush. I had to borrow boots One goal was the store in Goldpines five miles away (no such thing as a path) which nearly did me in. Bunty's tea and date squares supplied the energy for the return hike. There was a badminton court in the Hall where I had my hands full trying to beat Gladys, the local star. Remember…these were radio only days so entertainment was homemade.

  …In my description of the lay of the land I didn't mention a short land barrier across the water. Transportation of all kinds of supplies for communities further north had to be by water. In the summer boats of all kinds were pulled up and over this barrier by an overhead stretch of rail ruled by expert Lief Erickson who brooked no interference…a fun process to watch In winter loaded tractor trains drove across the frozen lake and up and over but there was always the threat of breaking through that temperamental ice.  Disasters had happened and there was no way to rescue the victims.

...I enjoyed spending time with the trim single teacher, well-versed in local lore.  In this area harvesting wild rice by boat in the swampy water was the right of the natives and the high price of this rarity source of some income.  I was fascinated when Grace showed me how much cleaning and washing the crop required...it seemed to go on for hours.  Grace was a great walker too and a good source of gossip.  We shared one special event in my second Spring Breakup trip in 1945.  I had been the first to hear over the radio about the death of Roosevelt...sadly before the end of the European war.  Victory did come soon after and once again I spread the news.  The teacher and I decided this required celebrating.  We contacted six ladies to bake cake layers in large jelly roll pans.  Others womped up the filling to pile up the layers.  Red, white and blue icing covered the top.  Happily someone had a batch of small Canadian flags for the final touch...what a splendid confection...ample for the whole colony to share.  Somewhere there is a black and white snapshot of everyone gathered around the masterpiece in the Hall and singing Oh Canada.  What a lovely colored digital memento that would have made.  Fortunately the "blower" didn't send a warning blast during the party because the one time that it had the hall was emptied of males in no time flat.  Keeping the Plant going was top priority.

...Yes, at Ear Falls I was on call 24/7 and mostly all was serene.  Besides the usual infections of all kinds, there were a few crises.  One was a chip of steel being embedded in a man's eye...safely removed and no infection blessedly.  Then the inevitable, in this case a native woman who had not left to have her baby.  Bunty Nicholls and I spent all one day consulting with the doctor by a very poor phone line and trying to engineer the strangling cord birth but the babe did not survive.  Happily the mother did.  I had on a brown skirt and a white apron and over those hours my perspiration transferred the dye to my apron.  Likely such a sad loss would not happen today.

...Having mentioned dear, calm, reliable Bunty seems a good moment for a capsule account of the two of them.  Ron had been a choir boy at Westminster Abbey as a lad in England and was in the first World War.  An injury resulted in a plate in his head and he had been advised to lead a quiet life.  Somehow that translated into storekeeper in the wilds of Ontario!  The Nicholls had trouble keeping the store shelves stocked what with helping out every stray hunter and fisherman who visited them regularly.  I remember seeing a pile of airmail letters an inch high that had come in one postal delivery ...all from the boys overseas who had received their parcels.  I also heard that after the war Ron and Bunty were cited by the Red Cross for their outstanding generosity.  Theirs was a small house which was also home to a St. Bernard dog who was as big as Ron. There was a picture of them on the cover of an American magazine showing the dog on his hind feet with front paws resting on Ron's shoulders. What a fascinating book their story would have made.

...And that just leaves the event that caps my Ear Falls adventure...this time due to Bill Dowd's stubborn streak. This was a Breakup run and I was just a tad too late. Ice was forming on the plane wings when I arrived and flying in was out. Not to let a little frozen water stop him Bill called me at the boarding house in Sioux Lookout and told me to dress the next morning in all my warm clothes and be ready early because he and Oscar Nymark would come out in the "Lollypop"...a sturdy steel boat whose accommodation was a central motor and two wooden benches. Bill realized he needed a pro and Oscar knew both the Lollypop and Lac Seul forward and backward. As for me...it was just another adventure and better than ignominiously heading back home on the next train.

My crew arrived on schedule bearing a wicker basket of sandwiches and a large thermos of coffee which seemed like a bit of overkill to me for a short trip. We set out in increasing cold and reached the Hudson Bay Trading Post at Osnaberg by noon. We would do the rest of the run in the afternoon. Not until later did I realize that I was seeing one of the last of the Trading Posts that had served the north for so many years, soon to disappear completely. The rugged factor met us along with his wife and I admired the sturdy log store and inside the beaver, muskrat and other pelts hanging on the walls. They, along with beaded moccasins and clothing, had been traded for the supplies on the shelves needed by the trappers. Aboard again at one point we pulled into land and I was given a flashlight and directed to plough through the snow and take care of my needs. Then the weather really socked in with howling winds and blinding snow. Soon darkness began to descend and it was obvious we wouldn't make it. Oscar found a safe cove and tied us up. I was given the top of the motor and the men took a bench each and after munching on the dwindling supply of sandwiches toasted over the oil lamp we retired to get what sleep we could, punctuated by snores. With daylight the Lollypop took off to make a dash across the remaining open water. That sturdy little boat bounced through the whitecaps and finally made it to the Ear Falls dock. A shout of welcome from the crowd that had gathered gave me my first inkling that this had been a close call. Standing on the dock I couldn't believe the tons of ice that blanketed every inch of that craft. We were assured that had we not made that successful final attempt the minus 30'Fahrenheit predicted would have frozen us into the lake that night. Thanks to Bill insisting on having Oscar do the job we had survived. Nevertheless he was given a severe "chewing out" for risking our lives on such a dangerous escapade.

I'm glad I didn't know any better and just enjoyed the trip. The whole story ended up in a book called "Yesterday the River".

I was privileged to experience Ear Falls as it was in those challenging days. I was almost disappointed to learn that they now have a stoplight at the dam…part of the highway that connects it to the outside world. Better of course all round but not nearly so excitingly adventurous!

Ron's lake boat transport to Port Arthur with his summer convention buddies in the 1960's

## 32. NEW YORK – NEW YORK

From the dusty attic to the chair with picture albums...to just a stash of memories.

From the northern bush to the jungle of a huge city. Adventures can be anywhere. In fact who would have thought in those early days of our shoestring incomes that the glamorous world-famous metropolis of New York would become an affordable destination. My very first venture came in 1947 when two Hydro friends Ev Cheney and Joyce Marsden...both executive secretaries at Hydro and good company...talked me into joining them for a Thanksgiving weekend holiday. We made a mixed threesome...Ev was a perky brunette and Joyce a self-assured blonde. I had to miss my niece's Baptism and also didn't have the cash but I couldn't resist. The family forgave me and with reckless abandon I got my first loan ever of $100 (train fare, hotel, food, unknown needs?)

Thanksgiving Friday the three eager beavers, one bag each, boarded the overnight train headed for the Big Apple. No funds for berths of course so we welcomed the pillows the cheerful porter handed out and curled up like pretzels into our seats. Unfortunately the pillows were taken back at the border. It was three rumpled, unwashed, grumbling travellers with cricks in their necks who arrived at crowded Grand Central Station in the morning...too bleary-eyed to appreciate its vaulted grandeur. We crammed into a yellow checkered cab and headed for our rooms at the Taft Hotel ($2.50 a night?). What luxury! Our own bathrooms and pillow-piled beds and those bulging extra doors in the middle of the regular ones that could hold clothes to be picked up...cleaned ...and returned. Not by us though. Re-energized we settled for a quick cleanup and then took off. Ahead were three full days on foot in perfect autumn weather to explore Manhattan.

We soon blended into the endless crowds of sometimes shabby but always to us sophisticated New Yorkers. Mouths permanently agape we took in the sights (not necessarily in this order)...staring first at the highflying skyscrapers. None of any account in Toronto yet. The enormous sparkling chandelier in the lobby of Radio City Music Hall led us to the theatre and the show with the lovely rockettes kicking their famous legs with military precision. Elevators like rockets ended at the viewing level of the Empire State building where Central Park was spread out below...its ponds and walkways waiting to provide a pleasant ramble. Rockefeller Centre impressed with its mini lake and gardens.

We could only picture the skating rink and the famous huge Christmas tree from Scandinavia. A boat tour around the island eased our complaining feet as we enjoyed a view across the water of the panorama on land. No United Nations towers as yet. The Statton Island Ferry was still the world's biggest bargain at 25cents…and over it all rose the brooding Statue of Liberty…icon for so many millions of immigrants to the U.S.A. The days were full.

Undoubtedly there was food demolished at regular intervals but only one left any impression…a treat in the posh hotel dining room accompanied by a band that was actually from Canada…not Guy Lombardo though who was booked into the Roosevelt for New Year's Eve in Times Square. What I have no memory of is of worrying about running out of funds. It would be an interesting project to price that trip by today's bloated standards.

Once again on Monday evening we boarded the familiar grubby CNR coach. We each had purposely saved enough to head for the dining car and toast our super successful holiday with one of those individual little cocktail bottles each that used to be dispensed…the extent of our souvenirs. No rest yet. From Union Station it was straight to the office to endure a full work day…all of it well worth the exhaustion, blisters and aches. By any standard we had thoroughly initiated New York. And this was only the intro to more trips to the Big Apple in the years ahead.

## 33. NEW YORK...A NICE HABIT

I am amazed now that in the Fifties we took occasional trips to New York for granted in spite of minimal funds. It was the entertainment centre of North America...and musicals were the entertainment passion of the day. "Oklahoma" hit a high that continued for the next few decades. Canada, and particularly Toronto for us, had excellent local theatre we could enjoy regularly...but the super song and dance shows were in a class of their own...thanks to the genius of Lerner and Lowe, Rogers and Hart and Hammerstein. Ed Mervish was still just piling up millions at his bargain basement store, Honest Ed's...although he may already have been dreaming of breaking into the theatre world by buying and restoring the Alexander Theatre down on King Street and surrounding it with his food emporiums jammed with antiques. Neither had Tyrone Guthrie yet been persuaded to take a chance and come over from England to colonial Stratford Canada and launch a successful Shakespearean venue. Meantime air fares to New York were so reasonable ($50 return or less?) they made it possible for fans to visit their American theatrical mecca.

Our first taste had been our drive from Niagara to New York after that "Lose the Bride" episode on May 5, 1951. Brother Larry was now established in his new position and undertook to add some glamour to our mostly hoofing-it sightseeing plans. We did have tickets to a show ("Guys and Dolls"?) and he treated us to dinner at Sardis, the popular pre-theatre restaurant. The staff was dedicated to getting their show-bound customers finished on time and would brook no dawdling over meals. Another day we were included in an invitation to cocktails at the apartment of business friends of Larry in a residential hotel facing Central Park. Ron and I found the building easily enough and looked around the lobby for the elevators. The doorman in his spiffy uniform politely asked for our host's name and then pointed us to their private elevator. We weren't too surprised to enter an elegant drawing room with windows looking out on Central Park. I couldn't help chuckling at the mental picture of our new house in Toronto perched in the middle with space to spare. The only fly in the ointment that trip was that I had neglected to bring anything but new trousseau shoes for which my feet paid dearly.

Remembering that ghastly train trip in 1947 it was blissfully exciting on our first flight to New York to go through the one and only exit at Malton Airport, walk across the field and climb aboard a Viscount with its propellers spinning, ready to roar down the runway. By the grapevine we had achieved a rather seedy but inexpensive hotel right downtown called the Iroquois. It was right next door to the famous Algonquin where the literary darlings of the Twenties such as Hemingway and Fitzgerald had hung out. I ventured a peek in but like ours it had come down in the world. My memory of our room was that the window was right next to the neon sign over the hotel entrance that blinked away all night. It mattered not a whit since we had tickets for "Brigadoon". They too had not skyrocketed as yet…we even thought $15 was a little steep.

Our outstanding achievement though was thanks to brother Larry. "My Fair Lady" with Julie Andrews, Rex Harrison and the incomparable Stanley Holloway of "Get me to the Church on Time" fame was taking Broadway by storm. With sisterly faith I wrote Bro and suggested that we would really like to see it. A week or so later we received back a telegram (remember them?) simply announcing that he had tickets for the week-end coming up only. Frantically we cancelled any dates, gathered our clothes and wallets and managed to book a flight. It was an unforgettably perfect evening. The musical faithfully followed Shaw's book "Pygmalion" and every piece of music was memorable. Larry did mention afterwards that he was staggered when he got the request and equally staggered when his frantic attempts were successful in view of sold-out performances. Even so I can't regret being so brash…and I don't think he regretted it either.

New York continuing to be possible for me was due to generous host brother Larry. He and wife Hilda and their family of four had settled into an imposing mansion in Lowden Woods, Rye, some miles north of the city in Connecticut. It had belonged to Manners Guru, Emily Post. His position as Vice President of Lever Brothers had lifted him to this financial level (albeit for just four years). The bit that lingers in my memory about the house was its huge ballroom. Emily had apparently built it to host theatricals. Hilda's large Indian carpet seemed stranded in the middle. It did make a great playroom for the youngsters and their friends from the private Country Day School they attended. And their home was a great place to visit. Public safety was still not in question and on my own I rode the overhead railway into town to meet Larry, passing through the miles of Harlem…the tenements so close to the railroad I felt I could lean out and touch the crumbling walls. In the heat of summer scantily-clad residents sat out on the fire escapes, smoking who knows what, drinking, fanning themselves and hoping for a breath of fresh air. Manhattan was neatly laid out and I had no trouble finding my way to shops or restaurants on various trips. I felt quite the sophisticated traveller.

Bro could have been absent for one of my visits but undertook instead to include me in a train ride to Washington with three business buddies.  I recall only that they treated me very warmly and that one of them was on his way to launch the first Minute Maid frozen orange juice on the market…a whole new concept.  We stayed at the Mayfair hotel and while my hosts were off wheeling and dealing I was left on my own to take in the sights.  It was 100' in the shade but I didn't seem to suffer as I clutched my city tourist map and covered block after block, admiring the White House, Congress, the Needle…exactly like but infinitely more impressive than their well-known pictures.   The gigantic figure of Lincoln seemed to brood over the city from his monument.  I loved it all.  Meandering alone is more rewarding than being herded on and off a bus, loaded with tourists while someone talks endlessly through a noisy mike.

New York was where I followed up some family clues.  I located the Donnell Branch of the New York Public Library, just across the street from the Museum of Modern Art…the plaque in the lobby verifying my information.  Another time I did a side trip to Albany, the capital city of the State.  There I was able to collect the few hundred dollars for each Dampier child, willed by our mother's great uncle Sheppard.  It hardly paid my expenses but was fun "closure" expedition.

Our last trek to New York was as part of a happy foursome including our dear friends Clara and Morley Thomas.  This time it was by car…a leisurely drive down through the lovely countryside past the Finger Lakes and along the Hudson River.  We had fallen for the report of some buddies about really reasonable accommodation in an "el cheapo" hotel close to the sights.  We were warned that the customers tended to be of the black and tan variety and we should take along some Dutch Cleanser since housekeeping service was iffy.  On the plus side, we could have a roomy suite with comfortable furnishings for a song.  As predicted it turned out to suit both our simple needs and slender budget perfectly.  Next door there was a Deli run by a cheerful Italian where we collected our daily sandwiches and milk for lunch.  For out tours we separated.  Clara would have none of the Empire State cum Rockefeller Centre routine so went off on her own to satisfy her more scholarly tastes.  At the end of the day we would meet to eat and then stretch out on our comfy furniture to share the day's adventures over a nog.  On the last day our Deli friend simply shook his head and handed us our lunch bags without being asked.  He could still not believe we only ordered milk.  On the last day of our drive back Morley, who had done a masterly job as our treasurer examined the remaining funds and announced we could celebrate with a good restaurant meal.  We didn't know then that we had also come to the end of New York bargain days.  We had made lots of deposits though in the Memory Bank.  Meanwhile while we were heading south for our entertainment Toronto, with Ed Mervish at the helm and his son following fast in his footsteps, had been developing into a world class theatrical centre.  We Canadians could now get our regular fixes at home.

However, should any readers want directions to enjoy the same spot in New York that we did, they need only find the Lincoln Centre. Where it stands now our holiday haven once stood.

The adult Dampier siblings 1960...youngest to oldest, Mary, Ted, Larry and Marjorie.

Cousins Dickie, Mary and Marjorie, in London Ontario in the 1980's.

## 34. TWO MARYS AND A VIOLET

I have one memento of this story that involved the three of us...a rhinestone maple leaf brooch that always brings it all back. It seems amazing now how unrelated strands combined over time leading to the climax.
   The Mathieson sisters were Violet and Mary (Mark 1)...eight and seven years older than brother Ron. Joining the family later made me Mary Mark 2. The girls graduated in the same mid-Twenties year from Trinity College, U. of T. Violet having missed a year due to a childhood illness. She became a popular High School teacher and apart from travels to her current school was a quiet homebody. After her father, dentist Dr. Will, died in the Thirties she became a support for (and under the thumb of) her strong-minded doctor mother, Dr. Lily, who took up a practice in Belleville leaving her children in the care of her mother. Mary was of a different metal...bright and attractive and among other things a very-talented pianist, she opted to work for Dr. Currelly at the Royal Ontario Museum. That was however a stop-gap until she could realize her dream of leaving this backward "colony" and escaping over to the Mother Country, England. I gather she had no compunctions about helping herself to anything handy that would further those plans. In the early Thirties she set sail, with the disapproval of her doting mother, joined by friend Henrietta. (A note: Henrietta's last name escapes me but she acquired a new one in England anyway when she met and married Dr.(Sir) Frederick Banting, the famous co-founder of Insulin. After losing him in 1941 she herself became a doctor in Canada and was a lecturer when I took a refresher course at Women's College Hospital some years later. More threads combining)  Arrived in England the friends parted and Mary set out to travel...over the years covering China, Africa from tip to toe, and several European countries, teaching English and working for the United Nations Relief and Rehabilitation Administration (UNRRA). This was the life that suited her wanderlust.
   Back home her family spent the war years and up to the Fifties waiting for Mary's blue Air Mail letters. Wouldn't Dr. Lily have feasted on worldwide E-Mails and pictures...even voice contact! In 1957 Violet had one of the complete two-week holidays at Christmas that happen every year now but then only occasionally. Mary was in Beirut, Lebanon, at the time...a city she described as the most beautiful she had ever seen. However, the Civil War which has ravaged that beauty ever since, had broken out. Mary planned to take a ship and holiday in Paris

and London before relocating and Violet decided this was an ideal time to catch up with her globe-trotting sister. Forthwith she bought an Air France ticket for the day her holiday started and then settled down to worry that unreliable Mary might not show up and she, Violet, would be stranded in a strange city. Ron solved that problem by playing White Knight and arriving home one day with a twin ticket for me. I was stunned but recovered to phone my friends and tell them I was spending Christmas in Paris this year…and that was NOT Paris, Ontario.

The unbelievable nature of air travel at that time began with Ron borrowing $800. That would cover the ticket and all expenses for the two weeks. My mental picture of Dr. Lily's dining room on the day of departure is like a scene from a farce. Violet had not as yet packed so rushed in with her empty suitcase and began jamming in her clothes. A friend sat at the table frantically sewing on some necessary garment. Dr. Lily, pale and wan, hovered about declaring that we must NOT cancel the trip just because she had just had a gall bladder op (they weren't today's quick variety) and had signed herself out of the hospital to be sure we got away. The suitcase was squeezed shut, fond farewells said and Ron just got us to the station in time to board the train for Montreal. (A note: Violet's choice of clothes worked like a charm and I didn't do so well with what I had packed so carefully). Now came an overnight stay with another friend in Montreal before finally taxiing to board our evening flight for Paris. Then came the luxury service applying even to economy passengers. Our dinner trays held Filet Mignon, delicious fixings and an exotic dessert prepared by the Ritz Carlton Hotel chef, accompanied by champagne on the house. Above our heads small hammocks were swaying, ready to receive traveling babies of which there were several. And they slept…as did we, soothed by our meal and the TLC of pillows and coverlets. All too soon came breakfast trays, six-hours ahead Paris time, followed by our arrival and reality.

A taxi of course…but how many franks does a taxi cost? Much fumbling with my unhelpful French/English dictionary. Was the driver thanking us for giving him too much or furious in French because we underpaid??? Never mind…Mary, in spite of a storm-tossed trip across the Mediterranean, was at the quaint hotel where she had booked our room on the Rue Mermoz. She was still an attractive very feminine red head who greeted us warmly and all was well.

Though this part is mainly an account of our trip it has a place in the story. Mary was obviously still leery of her "colonials". Watching the Parisian women on the streets I could agree that we had none of their sophisticated flair and style. Mary was a pleasant companion but didn't care to join our daily tourism. It was "Been there…done that" all the way. She filled her own days. Gradually though she began to enjoy our relaxed shoes-off sessions in the evenings when we chuckled over that day's adventures.

Note: Nobody at any time suggested that it was dangerous for two women to walk the streets of Paris alone.

Rather than the complete script of that wonderful first Paris/London holiday a listing of fun highlights will fill the bill:

...OUR DIGS...Mary did well. Our quaint Hotel Mermoz, not far from the Champs Elysees, was an unprepossessing four storeys with a tiny reception room at the front door and an "ascenseur" that clanked its way noisily as it rose. Strangely it would take us up to the top floor but we must walk down. Our bright main room slept us all with comfortable chairs to boot. The bath tub sported feet...toes and all...and needed a step stool to get in. Breakfast was included and delivered by pretty Lisette after an order had been called down. The first morning I undertook to show off my high school French..."trois petit dejeuners s'il vous plais" brought no response...but Mary l's "petit dejeuner pour trois" did the trick. Almost the same so why so fussy?

...STREET STROLLS...The area was a warren of crisscross streets full of intriguing shops and small restaurants. Violet and I set out on our first wide-eyed stroll and soon spotted some lovely hankies (yes...no Kleenex and we always used them and they made great gifts) in a shop window, planning to come back later. We never did find them again. It was a miracle we found our way back to the hotel. Mary had wisely visited a handy bakery and bought a loaf of...what else...French bread which customers tucked unwrapped under an arm. Another shop offered her an assortment of cheeses and milk. This she topped off with a bottle of wine from Cave Mermoz. We could lunch in our room by the window and enjoy the neighborhood sights. Venturing further afield I found an upstairs glove shop recommended by a friend back home and invested in a fine pair (gloves yet?). I even had the courage to fulfill my one dream of having an item of real French nighttime lingerie made to order. It was a once only lavish treat to be measured and treated like royalty. It would be ready another day. (Note: I wore the filmy gown until it almost fell apart and then sewed a copy myself). What a thrill to stroll by shops like Tiffanys and Cartiers. No going in...a snapshot of the signs was enough there.

...LANGUAGE AND GLITCHES...It was an adventure to find where to dine out. Menus in windows were little help so we chose one randomly. (remember, bilingual Mary was "Been there done that" still). The nice waiter soon twigged and brought his version of what we should order. Intrigued by the meat we tried saying "porc...boeuf?" to no avail. At last on some paper he drew a beast with antlers to show it was "venaison...a kind unavailable in Canada. Our next venture was the Metro subway which handily had a big map on the platform of destinations with lights that flashed including our choice...Versailles. We managed the tickets and the proper track but then hit a "rail" block. In vain we tried but drew only blank looks...until a bright soul realized we didn't know that "correspondence" meant "Go to the other side of the track". Versailles was achieved, gaped at in wonder and the return trip no problem.

Another glitch was our arriving for our first dinner at a restaurant at 6 p.m. There were few clients and the colonials (Mary 2's favorite word) ordered a drink, planning another before eating. The waitress ignored us until we managed to get her eye and order our meal. Back at the hotel Mary rolled her eyes and informed us that the French people went to a bar after work for an "aperitif"...then off home for a siesta before dining out no earlier than 9 p.m. Pre-dinner drinks were a NoNo but wine flowed as soon as the food was served. We admitted it was an improvement over the Canadian habit of too many quaffes over an hour or two before dining. We had a lot to learn from these civilized Parisians.

Next comes a change of pace so a good time to take a break ...but stay tuned. Bonne Chance!

## 35. CHRISTMAS IN LONDON

A "change of pace" took the form of a short flight from Orly across the channel to England (that elastic $800 again).  It was Christmas Eve and the dyed-in-the-wool Anglicans were determined to celebrate the Season at some Church of England.  With only an hour the flight attendants whipped up and down the aisles depositing snack trays and then swooping them up before smiling us off at our destination.  We headed for the Ecclestone Hotel in Chelsea where, wasting no time, we barely dropped our belongings before taking to the late afternoon streets, leaving Mary BTDT.  Violet was an ideal tourist companion…ready for anything and quick with a laugh.    Before we knew it up loomed Westminster Abbey as darkness fell.  No service there until the next day .    Unlike spread-out Canada history confronted us at every turn.  Trafalgar Square was next on the Agenda so we hopped on a bus indicating it was headed there…only to have the bus driver promptly tell us to hop back off and walk since it was a scant two blocks away.  A gentleman bus driver?  Sure enough there was Nelson's Monument with pigeons swooping, Christmas carols blaring and crowds of people in a holiday mood.
   We were on a roll.  "That's got to be St. Martin-in-the-Fields across there" I cried.  It was indeed and its own crowd was lining up outside the doors.  Over we hiked to find that only church members with tickets would be admitted to the midnight service at 11 p.m.   No revellers welcome.  We might as well join the line since we were on this roll we agreed.  Just being there was a thrill and we chatted happily with fellow queue members.  By mutual consent we stretched our story slightly to include having come all the way from the colony of Canada just to go to this service.  Mary's word came in handy.  When the doors finally opened two tickets had somehow been thrust in our hands and we were carried along in the crowd streaming into the church and up into the gallery.  Then I gasped…starched white uniforms rustled from all sides as nurses from all the London hospitals took their places in the nave to officiate at the service.   What a bonus for the delighted nurse from Canada who especially noted the frilly caps of famous St. Thomases Hospital.   Out again at 2 am. we dazedly set out on foot for the hotel…no taxis and we were starving.  The kind hotel doorman gave in to our pleas and managed to rustle up two small sandwiches before we fell into bed.

"Merry Christmas" carolled Mary at 8 a.m....an unwelcome awakening. She knew we had to breakfast and gather our kits to move over to Crosby Hall. Through the University Women's Club Violet had managed to book us into their much less expensive sleeping quarters. We were greeted there by the prim smiling Warden (Den Mother?) as we gaped at the huge vaulted hall of what had been the home of Sir Thomas More who had lost his head for disagreeing with his monarch. Henry VIII's portait loomed overhead. Our accommodations were another story...no attempt to impress there. Long utilitarian halls of basic rooms with cots had been tacked on the mansion. Heat required crawling into the cupboard to feed the hungry metre with shillings. Breakfast was toast and jam with an orange rolling around on a tin tray carried by a strapping maid who cheerfully announced "It coom like a miracle!" in true Brit style. The bathroom window was open to the frigid foggy elements. Closing it was useless only calling for the next user to reopen it. Well...we hadn't booked Buck House!

Being Christmas afternoon Violet and I headed for Westminster Abbey for their service and were on time to see and hear the costumed trumpeters in the gallery as they accompanied the Queen's speech from Sandringham. We enjoyed the service from chairs with cushion kneelers on the floor but did wonder why the choir boys stared at us as they processed down the aisle at the end. Apparently our colorful Canadian Christmas corsages were not in style in England. Back at the Hall we warmed ourselves with the sherry always available and set out again to sight-see. After several forays and tipples we dubbed ourselves "religious alcoholics"! On the last return we found tea and goodies being served at this quite late hour so we ate heartily as our last nourishment for the day. Only to find that Christmas dinner would be served at 9 p.m., preceded by the Warden's sherry party which we bipassed and had no trouble doing justice to the traditional turkey feast ending with blazing plum pudding. Though beautifully decorated the Great Hall was as usual damply chilly. The elderly Englishwoman at our table, huddled in a wool shawl and knitted wristlets, commented, "I understand that Canada is a teddibly cold country!" And here we were, longing for our good old central heating to warm our shivering bodies. Just the same we were enthralled by the fascinating mix of visitors from so many Commonwealth countries, like us, taking advantage of this exalted piece of history. Note: Remember that this is an account of our personal adventures...not the wonders of the Abbey, Crosby Hall or other sights replete with history.

Boxing Day held more surprises. We had the usual list of tourist sights to cover and set out eagerly after our "miracle" breakfast. As always Mary had seen it all. Clutching our maps we soon became aware of an eerie silence in the great city of London. Instead of being the Mad Shopping Day we expected everything was closed up tight, We soon found that there was only one drugstore open in the centre of the city, with all other merchandise fenced off even there.  Getting an aspirin which Violet needed became a challenge.  Our goal was the famous Madame Tussaud's Waxworks but flagging a taxi was a problem.  The cabbies were obviously enjoying a Boxing Day sleep-in.  Eventually a car did stop and, jumping out, the driver sporting a huge drooping red mustache inquired our destination and forthwith drove us to the door.  With true English hauteur he brushed aside our inquiry about the fare.  Seems this was Lord Somebody's shining Rolls Royce and he was the chauffeur doing his good Christmas deed.  We had wondered about the silver fittings and plush carpeting.  It was an exhilarating adventure which sadly was not repeated.  The waxworks didn't disappoint us though including the Chamber of Horrors which appealed more to Violet.  The Commonwealth display sported a new John Diefenbaker and behind him a sign saying "Mr. St. Laurant, removed for alterations."  We did wonder what they were doing to our poor Prime Minister.

  London came back to life the next day and we joined the bargain-seekers on festive, packed Oxford Street.  I was just going to buy a souvenir at one store and suddenly missed my camera.  I was panic-stricken.  The solemn-faced clerk sent me off to my last stop where the salesman announced that he had already sold my camera.  Enjoying my horrified reaction he produced it, poker-faced.  Racing back to the salesman down the street I found that he had waited patiently to complete my purchase.  Were all English salesmen that politely honest??  Probably not today.

  Our touristing continued in the few days left before our return to France.  A few notes only:  The past of The Tower of London was too much for history teacher Violet in spite of the jolly Beafeaters and the Crown Jewels.  I had to take her to the nearest pub to recover.  One virtue of the bombing of so many surrounding buildings was that it had opened up a better view of St. Paul's Cathedral...the empty craters a grim reminder still.  We even joined the lineup to see Agatha Christie's famous "Mousetrap", then in its 6th year and I believe still going strong today.  More than the play I remember the constant coughing by all the lungs weakened by the damp chill climate, and the air blue with cigarette smoke.     At intermission trays of food were passed along the rows to much clatter and chatter...  more like a pub than a theatre...great fun but not exactly high drama. Another stop was the famous Antelope restaurant for traditional roast beef and Yorkshire pudding.  Getting to the "Ladies" meant treading around all the swains quaffing their pints seated on the stairway, unfazed by all those silk legs.  And much more but not here.

  The flight back to Orly seemed even more frantic.  It felt like home to the threesome as we rattled up in the trusty lift to our sunny hotel room.  Mary had relaxed more and more as the days passed and was obviously sad at the impending parting. The last Must Do in Paris was for us all to be on the Champs Elysee for New Year's Eve. We managed a late dinner at a favorite restaurant and waited with the excited crowd of customers for their clock to strike midnight. Bells whistles and fireworks erupted on cue and the chef leaped across a counter to kiss a pretty waitress. We headed for the street to join the dancing singing revellers. A handsome man grabbed Violet and kissed her soundly exclaiming, "I came here from America to kiss a lovely French Mademoiselle." "And I was looking for a handsome Frenchman." giggled Violet in return.

It was sad to see Mary standing alone as we waved from the Departure lounge. The flight home not only turned the clock back six hours but we had no tail wind. The 13 hours seemed endless. The gratis half bottle of champagne with our meal turned into two full bottles for me. Violet fell asleep and the couple ahead of us didn't want any. Wisely I didn't try to take up the slack. Sleepless I watched the lights of Greenland twinkle below in the darkness. This time meals were too many hours apart. Finally arrived at Malton Airport the frozen plane doors had to be thawed out. Just as well we had not had an emergency landing on the way. By now numb with fatigue we tottered off across the tarmac...only to see on the roof of the airport a huge banner held up in the morning sunshine by a welcoming group of dear friends..."Bienvenue Violette et Marie". Our fatigue vanished as we hugged all round and then made our way back to 5 Northglen for a breakfast of pancakes, syrup, sausages and orange juice that had an odd alcoholic flavor. How Violet managed to get to school the next day I'll never know since I was numb throughout.

The surprising epilogue to that trip was that sister Mary must have decided that "colonial" no longer applied to her sister and sister-0in-law. She decided to make a trip home the next summer after an absence of over twenty years. Dr. Lily was of course ecstatic and the family proceeded to plan a happy homecoming. The new Mary, happy to be home, spent time with us at 5 Northglen and being chauffeured around the city. She couldn't believe how Toronto was now so cosmopolitan. Dr' Lily's contribution was a wildly erratic scenic drive around the Belleville countryside. One surprise was that Mary announced she was going to be married and spent time browsing through Morgan's and Holt Renfrew in search of a trousseau. Sister Violet was skeptical since Mary had been engaged several times in the past, none of them ending in a wedding. Altogether it was a most successful two week reunion before Mary1 made the return flight to England.

A couple of weeks later we were listening to the radio news and heard that a BOAC plane had collided with a small plane over Anzio in Italy on its way to Rome, with the loss of all aboard. Not long after, the dreaded knock came to Dr. Lily's door. Mary and her fiance (also a

Canadian) were aboard on their way to Rome to be married. We were all struck dumb.   The next few weeks were a nightmare while Ron contacted the airline and undertaker in England. while we waited in a kind of limbo for the coffin to arrive for the funeral.   It was such a heartbreaking end after having Mary return to the family fold.   We could only be grateful for the new happy memories.  Those were the days too before lawsuits and settlements.   It didn't occur to us to ask for anything more than just sending her home.

No I haven't forgotten the maple leaf pin.  I had taken it over as a gift for Mary.  She was wearing it on the plane and it was returned to me.  Every now and then I get it out and look at it and remember how those many strands had met and connected.  But I just can't bring myself to wear it.

## 36. MAJESTY

Royalty…His Royal Highness…Your Majesty. This is not a very popular topic in these republican-minded days but those were magic words in my growing up years when Canadians were rooted in the monarchy. In fact as children we didn't know or care in the slightest that we could not even use that word officially. We were British subjects and our country just a colony of the great worldwide British Empire. George V looked benignly down on his subjects from every official wall in town. The Red Ensign, really meant only to fly from the masts of the British Navy was our flag with just a small Coat of Arms added. 24$^{th}$ of May holidays in honor of a Queen long dead were our favorites…"The 24$^{th}$ of May, The Queen's birthday, If they don't give us a holiday we'll all run away!" How proud my friend Clara and I were, our dresses draped in red, white and blue bunting, to lead our Grade 3 class in the school parade down the main street of Strathroy, marching to the roll of drums, headed for the Fairgrounds and the celebrations.. But wait…my memory tells me that a louder roll was not drums, it was thunder! Soon the rain had turned us red white and blue all over. After the tears that joined the downpour that year, cake and ice cream revived our royal spirits.

To us Empire-breds things were fine as they were. Nevertheless Canadian citizenship came first with our own passports and finally in 1965 we could fly our own Maple Leaf flag. There was quite a national free-for-all choosing the design and I must admit I wanted blue stripes at the sides to represent "from sea to sea" but that design lost. Along the way the die-hard royalists became proud Canadians too. However, more than with younger generations, the magic of the Royal Family still persists. Queen Elizabeth11 has visited us over forty times and you can be sure that a big percentage of the flag-waving crowds have been around as long or longer than she has. We want to keep her thank you.

All of which leads to some extra connections with royalty through husband Ron's particular talents. He had caught the eye of Bob Saunders …ex-Toronto mayor and now Chairman of Ontario Hydro and very fond of instigating public shows. Ron's first taste of his new role came one day with a phone call from Saunders asking him to spend the next couple of days showing the sights including Niagara Falls to a visitor. To Ron's surprise the Royal in the limousine that picked him up was Prince Akahito, heir to the Japanese throne. (Today he is the aging monarch with his own son waiting in the wings). The Prince spoke perfect English and was an interesting and enthusiastic companion. At the end of the tour the limo simply dropped the Prince off at the Royal York as he bowed his thanks in true Japanese style.

Let there be a special event to plan and Ron was Bob's man. Saunders was also Chairman of the annual Toronto Exhibition and the first royal to need Ron's expertise was Princess Margaret. That year a beautiful new fountain dedicated to Her Royal Highness turned the central square of the grounds into a rainbow waterfall. The Princess was typically late arriving for the ceremony but my equally royalist pal Alice and I loved just sitting in the crowded bleachers in anticipation. The Queen's sister was indeed lovely and the wait was well worthwhile. The most fun though was the motor cavalcade of VIPs. Ron might have been in the tag end automobile but he bowed his head, smiled and waved with the best of them for the benefit of his fans in the crowd.

Next in line was the opening in 1954 of the new Hydro Electric plant in Niagara Falls with Princess Marina, the Duchess of Kent ,the on-the-spot celebrity. Arrangements began many months ahead including a trip to Canada by the Duchess's personal secretary…a very pleasant, real pucka (it's in the dictionary) Brit…to consult with Ron. After one busy morning in The Falls Robert suggested they should go to the nearest pub for a pint and lunch. Ron was horrified and tried to explain the nature of a pub in Canada but to no avail. In they marched to a gloomy smoke-filled room crowded with workmen. Ron quickly wiped a table clear of beer stains with his handkerchief while his unconcerned guest waited to lay out his supply of post cards to send home. Ron's furtive peek showed that two of them were addressed to young Prince Charles and Princess Anne at Buck House. Ron refused to remember what was rustled up for their lunch!

The Royal party included the pretty teenage daughter of the Duchess…Princess Alexandra. She had the fresh peaches and cream English complexion and spirit of fun. We met her at a welcoming luncheon where she enthused about the beautiful countryside along the Niagara Parkway. Alexandra also giggled over the fun she had with the staff, playing tricks like apple-pieing beds in the privacy of their whole floor of the Sheraton Brock Hotel.

The big excitement for me was when we were tapped at the final reception to go up and meet the Duchess personally and receive an autographed picture. I was somewhat mortified when Ron had to haul me away from extending my allotted time for chatting with the Duchess. The picture is still a treasure that any young friend just looks at and says …"Who on earth is that?" I also saved a little packet of the elegant letters and envelopes that had arrived from the royal residence over those special months.

I have to be satisfied now with my copies of Majesty magazine that keep me up with the (less lurid?) events of royalty but especially with our splendid 87-year-old Queen and her crusty consort Prince Philip. I even had a letter to the editor published when I was giving beleaguered Prince Charles some support a few years back. Whatever their ups and downs members of "The Firm" are still warmly welcomed by Canadians and hopefully always will be.

    We are just as anxious to welcome the new Prince/Princess as the Brits!

# Stories of My Century

Princess Marina, The Duchess of Kent, definitely the Star of that era. This picture a treasure to be given me.

### 37. THE UCHI LINE

Apart from colonies like The Canyon there were other areas of isolation in the Ontario Northland that looked to the Hydro nurse for a helping hand. One was called The Uchi line where those giant towers carrying the electricity stretched over fifty miles or so of particularly desolate bush land. At every 12 miles along the way was a small snug log house in a clearing fenced against the wild denizens that lurked in the woods around them. For each of those linemen the isolation was complete. Their job was to walk or snowshoe along the Line six miles in each direction every week to check out any problems. They would plan to meet their counterpart coming the other way from the next stop.. At regular intervals a bush plane would drop down at each house and deliver provisions, mail and anything they may have ordered the last time but otherwise the linemen existed alone. At least we could be sure there were no mothers needing help with the arrival of her baby!

The only solution to the physical and mental effects of such a life was a visit from "Outside" like the nurse. On my winter trip I was armed with some treats, prescribed medications, reading material and a cheerful friendliness. My mandate was to assess each situation for any problem that needed further help. The tour began with the familiar train ride that had set me on my way to Ear Falls. This time I stepped down sooner at Nakina, thankfully in daylight. Small wonder if few had ever heard of this rail metropolis with its little red station, small boarding-house-hotel and several shacks. Bundled against the cold and blizzarding snow I was delighted to see a pleasant parka-clad young man jumping off too. The crusty station master led us and our baggage to the boarding house and announced that meals were available at the station only. No one else was in residence. Not to worry since it was a short stop and I would be off on my tour the next day. Meantime Bob's company was welcome and we amused ourselves by slogging through the snow along the road which ran parallel to the track in each direction. No need to decide how far to go since it ended a quarter of a mile each way. Then we needed to struggle out to the air strip and hangar to check arrangements for our plane ride. The pilot in his shanty grinned a welcome with the news that the weather was about to sock in and we would just have to wait out the storm.

How many games of gin rummy and how many meals of eggs, canned beans and hash and how many rugged trips to check the plane plans could we handle? Phoning in my predicament to Head Office only produced raucous laughter at the other end. For four days the stranded travelers played cards and trudged hopefully out and unhappily back. I was just glad to have a companion who was pleasant, had cards and spoke English!

    At last we whooped for joy as on our early morning approach to the hangar we heard the plane revving up. In we piled and I sat with the pilot since Bob was leaving us at the first stop. Never did know his job. My eyes were always glued to the postage-stamp-sized spot pointed out as our next landing strip…as always the wizard pilot zoomed in right on..

Without fail there was a bearded bundled-up body waving us in. Over many mugs of tea I spent as long as possible at each stop to hear the litany of problems, make notes and dispense my goodies. The gratitude was heartwarming, making me wish I could do it more often and stay longer. It made the trip particularly important in that I decided one of the men would have to be replaced to preserve his health.

    The plane made its last landing at Pickle Lake where two families lived with children being home-schooled by their active young mothers…what saintly women they were in my eyes. Looking around I could imagine what a lovely spot it would be in the summer with a shimmering lake and teeming river to swim and boat in…albeit with lots of mosquito goo and for a limited time. I was impressed that this group seemed quite content with their lot for however long it was. We feasted on potatoes and venison and pie before a friendly sendoff back to Nakina. By the way I was seriously "skunked" at rummy by Bob!

    Today the houses are abandoned and the lines are efficiently kept in repair electronically. I'm just glad I had the chance to meet those rugged northern Canadians. There are still jobs to be done by men, without technology, in the far lonely north and we can be proud of them as they do their bit to keep our country "strong and free".

## 38. DICKIE

A few special people need their own space in my past. One is my cousin Dickie English. Dickie and her mother (Aunt Olive) were the dear souls who provided me with the Teen Treat of a trip to Chicago when I was just 16...as I have already recounted. Dickie is just a shadowy memory from those childhood Sunday afternoons when I was in public school. She had trained as a teacher in Strathroy but given it up and I suspect one reason was that she didn't have much use for kids in general and her boisterous Dampier cousins in particular. By nature Dickie craved adventure so moved in with Chicago relatives in about 1930 and found a business job. Later the West beckoned and she became involved in World War 11 while working for an American army officer in the western States. I believe they were engaged but never married and the lovely diamond ring my cousin left me in her will was likely her engagement ring. She never did confide any details of that part of her life. I was never told how she acquired that nickname though since she had been christened Olive after her mother. "Olives are in the bottom of a martini glass" she stated firmly. Dickie it was.

My cousin's final move was to San Francisco where she opened her own stenographic business in one of the downtown towers. This made it possible for her to continue caring for her mother but lack of real financial security prevented this talented woman from reaching her full potential, as some kind of writer...probably a full-time journalist. Dickie did have articles published in the prestigious Atlantic Monthly magazine and elsewhere. My first contact with her on my own was when we became letter buddies in spite of eleven years difference in age. I always looked forward to those fat envelopes plopping through my mailbox. For any young readers, letters were a form of communication that preceded E-Mail and Facebook. Dickie had a wide range of friends in the artistic world of San Francisco and was a fixture in her particular seat at the San Francisco Opera. Her apartment on Russian Hill had actually withstood the earthquake back at the beginning of the century. It provided a view of the island of Alcatraz from its front door near the top of the street. This was a fascinating eclectic part of downtown where the mix of neighbours came to respect and look after the safety of the woman with the aristocratic profile, her hair in a neat bun over each ear, who was recognized by her large black felt hat in the winter and white one in the summer. Dickie was a great conversationalist and her ready wit had won her many friends. Visiting her was always an exciting glimpse of life in a fascinating city.

There are others but my first Dickie anecdote happened long before I made my first trip. . She was a member of the English Speaking Union. During the war many foreign ships anchored in the busy harbour and one weekend it was a British battleship. Members of the E.S.U. were expected to entertain the officers for a day and Dickie found three had been assigned to her for one Saturday, She was stunned not having a mansion with a pool and other amenities as other well-heeled members had. In desperation she called her rather eccentric friend Cary Baldwin who just happened to be curator of the San Francisco Zoo and told him her problem.

"Not to worry Dickie...you bring the food for a light dinner" said relaxed Cary, "I'll provide the entertainment."

So, having greeted her spiffy white-uniformed and bemedalled guests at her apartment, Dickie, the officers and the provisions were on their way. It was a pleasant meal during which Cary's pet llama wandered about greeting the guests with a slobbery lick. When it was dark, Cary disappeared, then returned, dramatically strapping on a holster and guns and rattling the Zoo keys since it was now closed to the public. Fingers to lips he cautioned his guests to be very quiet and led the way directing his flashlight in the pitch dark. Noisily the gate was unlocked, bringing forth the most blood curdling screams from the nearest cage, apparently housing the zoo's most humongous gorilla. When their hair had stopped standing on end the little safari was led into a huge building also in pitch darkness. Suddenly the lights came up. "Watch out" yelled Cary, and there was a line of enormous elephants, trunks extended to snatch the loaves of bread which Cary was tossing in rapid succession at the officers. The pachyderms obviously intended to pick up any of the men who didn't part with their catch fast enough. There were no casualties. Less hair-raising were the visits to the monkey island with the air full of chatter and screams, the koala bears in their eucalyptus trees and the swooping and twittering of hundreds of winged creatures in the enormous bird sanctuary. Delighted with the tour the group was ready to leave when an employee came with an emergency call for Cary. "Come along with me to the animal operating room." Cary beckoned. They did...and with eyes popping watched a huge lioness top their super show off by having a hysterectomy. The San Francisco Chronicle next day featured "the sensational entertainment provided by a tweedy spinster from the English Speaking Union with the unlikely name of Olive English!" One reason that I can tell this story in such detail is because my sister Marjorie and I enjoyed the exact same adventure (minus the hysterectomy) on one of our visits. Like the sailors we loved it!

My solo visits to San Francisco started in the Fifties. I enjoyed joining the mixed "salon" of Dickie's interesting friends and went with her to see many of the fascinating sights and to eat in some of the intimate small restaurants in that cosmopolitan city. Dickie's apartment was roomy and cosy and with a fine view of now vacant Alcatraz out in the sparkling Pacific...far enough from shore to have prevented any escaped inmate from making it to land. Dickie's particular bachelor friend George, an easy going business associate had become the organizer of a group of three or four friends who had made themselves her protectors. Considering the dubious character of many of the inhabitants of that downtown area (she detected the odor of pot smoking coming up from the apartment below for instance) she needed it. He had a key to her digs and often welcomed whoever was available for the frequent Happy Hour gab fests while they waited for her. It was a very knowledgeable lot and I could enjoy the talk even if I couldn't keep up with American politics and the economy. It was just a short relaxing time before dinner at the end of a busy day.

At the bottom of the street was a favorite but not very prepossessing eatery easy to reach on foot. Inside, a bar stretched down one side. On the other was room for three square tables with simple plastic cloths each seating eight. The routine was simply to be ushered to a seat by the robust black-haired and gimlet-eyed hostess and wait for the table to fill with customers. Everyone then introduced him or herself. There were middle-aged regulars from across town and strangers of all ages and sex from far and wide...a very presentable group. A smiling aproned waitress dealt out bowls of steaming pastas, veggies and salads to be ladled on to waiting plates ourselves. By that time conversation was lively and a pleasant party in the making. The proprietress quietly policed her domain even as she smilingly welcomed her guests. One night a bleary-eyed drunk came staggering through the door only to find himself about-turned with a "No you don't Buster" and on his way back out on the double! No bouncer needed. At the end of one visit Dickie and I were so enjoying our chat with the lad next to us that we invited him to walk up the hill with us for a nightcap. We felt quite secure. Her large floppy white hat in the summer and black one in the winter made her recognized and protected.

We spent many happy hours touring about, sharing a sense of humor about life's vagaries and the people and sights we encountered. Who would not remember boarding the graceful 65-foot sailing ship Good News recently bought by some of Dickie's well-heeled friends from the Wurlitzer family (still wealthy when their machines were going out of style), sailed from New York around through the Panama Canal and up to its new home. We raced a sister craft out under the Golden Gate Bridge with sails billowing in the ocean breezes while we enjoyed a lavish on-deck feast. It was a thrilling adventure (Of course I thought:

"If my friends could just see me!). On another occasion Dickie and I boarded a ferry to cross the bay to Sausalito and decided to enjoy the trip up front on the deck...only to be drenched by an unexpected mighty wave that reduced us to dripping hysterics. On shore we repaired to a bar for a sandwich lunch and were laughing over a restorative cocktail when the bartender with a flourish produced refills. "Two ladies who are enjoying themselves so much deserve a treat" he smiled as he poured! We had not intended the extra so we lingered over our lunch to prepare ourselves for a more conservative return trip!

My cousin lived until her eighties, lovingly cared for by friends. The San Francisco Chronicle featured her passing as a well known figure in the city's opera world with a lengthy article. On a voyage to the East Dickie had acquired a handsome oriental brocade silk gown which became her trademark as she sailed down the aisle to her long-held seat during the Opera Season each year. Her absence brought forth many tales from the audience that had come to know her and regret her passing.

By just being her intelligent, smiling, entertaining self my cousin had won a niche in San Francisco.s history.

Elegant cousin Dickie holding court in San Francisco...1960-70's.

Dickie's mother, our Aunt Olive, always in the background working and helping others. Dickie cared for her until the end.

## 39. THE DRAMA GUILD OF CANADA

If you are wondering why you have never heard of this organization not to worry. There is not and never was a Drama Guild of Canada...at least until a group of friends initiated it on November 25, 1954, at the home of Morley and Clara Thomas in Toronto...having made sure of that fact. (The bracketed names are only for those involved.)

There was a reason. This was when TV was taking the Canadian public by storm. At an earlier gathering there had been a heated discussion among this group of like-minded friends (including the Thomases, Bert and Ruth Longmire, Ron and Mary Mathieson, Miriam Morrow and Joan Brown) on the subject of wasting what had once been pleasant social evenings by being forced to sit throughout with eyes glued to a screen. Clara and Ron took charge, suggesting that all present form a play-reading group with monthly meetings at members homes. Joan would use her library contacts to acquire copies for all of whatever play the host/hostess chose. This would be kept secret with the one rule that no one would read the play ahead of time. Parts would be assigned at the meeting...a strange arrangement that provided much hilarity. Try ad libbing a part from Shakespeare for instance. The clueless thespians were left to stumble through their parts. Stars were definitely not born.

Little did we know that we had just grasped the tail of a tiger. As of this writing I have just received from Morley an 8-page closely typed listing of the activities of this group and the other chums who joined its ranks over the years (Kay Liddy, John and Pat Morrow, Mary and Ari van Rijns, Lorna and Luke Irwin, Alicia Forgie, Jean Shaw. Dorothy and Alec Black and Larry Dampier were "far flung" out-of-town members) and it is mind-boggling. Only a condensed account is possible here. Out of interest how many years did this "Guild" survive? The last recorded event was on October 20, 1973, making it almost twenty years. One amazing fact is that all remained friends to the end...quite an achievement for any assembly of humans.

Play-reading soon morphed into a desire to use their own talents by means of skit nights a couple of times a year. The Mathieson downstairs recreation room became "Guild Hall" and the adjoining furnace room the change room and repository of props. Joan Brown demonstrated a hitherto unknown skill at producing a program for each event having bullied the members into submitting their titles on time. A quick survey brings the count to 13 skit nights. But wait a bit...the tiger was in full flight and several offshoots found their way to the Activities

Calendar.  "Mathiesons Muster" was the designation of group treks to the Mathieson vacation spot on Bass Lake that fortunately had enough space for many bodies to bed down.  The list includes six of these efforts.  Then there were several mass migrations to Stratford performances via the Blackburn swimming pool in London...an almost disastrous plan which nearly had the tickets tossed in favour of more feasting and water sports.  The plan was to "plaque up" a chair at the theatre in Stratford being constructed to replace the tent...to be a memento from a fellow acting group.  The money somehow got lost under the dining room carpet of the current secretary...no use trying to explain that one.

Further perusals of the listing reveal two minstrel shows where Bert, Morley and Ron made hilarious "end men", adlibbing their banter like pros...several complete shows by the talented and musical Longmires...equally talented evenings by Lorna and Alicia...not to forget a series of New Year's celebrations at the Morrows with Ron always the designated driver and delighted when pulled over by a suspicious cop!

Too many to mention were the once-only events like the congratulation party for Clara at the Engineers Club on publishing a book...the homecoming party for return of Mary and Violet from Paris and London...the tree trimming for the Mathiesons one Christmas...a trip to McMichael's Gallery in Kleinberg...an Election Party engineered by Steve and John Thomas at the Thomases with multi posters...a Potlatch planned by Joan...a Scottish Ceilidh for Susan Longmire and beau Ian...and too many more to mention.  Here are a few highlights

...The unforgettable "Harrowing School" skit by Lorna and Alicia...taking place at the school attended by the children of one-eyed Saxons wounded at the Battle of Hastings...all members wearing black eye patches.

...Among the hilarious moments...Bert suffering through a heat wave with his feet in a bucket of water.

...Very pregnant Pat Morrow in a striped shirt and husband John padded out and in an identical outfit doing a joint act.

...Joan Brown doing Winnie the Pooh.

...A Mathieson Muster with Ron as Father Brebeuf in sackcloth and hood marching up and down the dock wielding a huge wooden cross and intoning who knows what while the brides of New France chugged around the point, Violet with blackened teeth.

Over the years since the D. G. of C. members have frequently reminisced and agreed that we were incredibly fortunate to have been part of such a super group.  All things come to an end but some leave a much bigger gap than others.

As a welcome postscript to this story: my friend Steve Thomas has endowed a seat at the Stratford Festival in the name of The Drama

Guild and arranged for a plaque to be installed on the seat at the Stratford Festival theatre.  Steve (son of Drama Guild member Morley Thomas), grew up a great admirer of his parents' group "The Drama Guild of Canada", even though they kept him awake many a night.

The following is a message sent to Steve from the Stratford Festival office; "Mr. Thomas...Christine Seip passed along your request to have a seat endowed here at the Stratford Festival.  I have reserved seat #59, Row D, Aisle 7.  I have placed the order for the seat endowment plaque and this is the layout...In Fond Memory of The Drama Guild of Canada, 1954 to 1973."

Having followed through with the endowment, our Drama Guild benefactor Steve Thomas is now entitled to be addressed as The Keeper of the Chair".

Memento of Stratford Ontario Festival Theatre in the tent, it's first year...1953

## 40. ARCADIAN COURT

The names "Robert Simpson Company" and "Arcadian Court" were once as well known to Torontonians as the now defunct "T. Eaton Company". The two competing stores were across the street from one another…each with their faithful clients. In the middle of the Twentieth Century it was impossible to imagine that they would not only be gone but their former existence unknown to a whole new generation.

A recent revamping of the Arcadian Court restaurant did not come near to achieving its former glory by all accounts. I can still picture that huge vaulted room with a surrounding balcony upstairs where females were only allowed if escorted by a male. No women's lib there. At one end downstairs was a handsome pillared stage from which fashion shows could be launched on the long runway…or a speaker or other entertainment provided. A sea of tables decked in fine white linen and floral centerpieces set the stage for the Spring luncheon parties and fashion shows that were part of the social calendar. We would stand gaping at the stunningly colorful effect of a sea of that year's flowered hats. No one would consider wearing last year's. Soft music by a string quartet mingled with the buzz of several hundred ladies clad in their best and relishing the Court's famous chicken pot pie and fruit pastry dessert. It was good to know that we could count on enjoying it all again next year…and those following…couldn't we?

Now it is better to remember than risk going back and suffering a noisy steel and plywood replacement.

### 41. A MOVING DISASTER...A MINI STORY

Anybody who has ever moved house...and who hasn't in this peripatetic age...has tales about unexpected, undesired glitches. One of mine had to do with a common complaint...how to get rid of the piles of books that they no longer wanted.

When Violet and I transferred from our houses in Toronto to living together she had a splendid plan that worked like a charm. Being a grad of Trinity and a teacher/librarian to boot she belonged to "Friends of the Library" at the College. As a fundraiser, books are collected by volunteers year-round and stored until their huge annual book sale. We simply contacted them and Jim, a well-organized friendly man, appeared at each of our places with his roomy station wagon and proceeded to pack it full of the loot. Without a doubt the simplest part of our move.

Come time to pack up once more for our exit to Napanee we set the same plan in motion. For some reason there was trouble locating transport but finally the same volunteer was rounded up. The books were in piles in the recreation room ready for boxes. I had even found one and filled it. On the appointed day I greeted Jim who had aged considerably and was obviously less limber. His wife had joined the trek but stated firmly that she would remain in the front seat. For his part her husband eyed the mountain of books and asked where the boxes were. I was stunned. "Boxes?" I mumbled, "Didn't you bring boxes????" "I can't carry them any longer like this so I'll be going" Jim replied heading back for the car. I was jolted into action. "Wait...I have boxes" I cried and headed for the furnace room with its metal shelves holding rows of boxes neatly filled and labelled with all our miscellaneous belongings...Christmas decorations, grandchildren toys, bathroom supplies, etc. One at a time I hauled them out, dumped them on the floor and rushed to the book room. I filled them and helped Jim lug those heavy loads to the car. The scowling wife kept muttering about the need to hurry. Fortunately, using every box took care of the job. As I shoved the last one in who should leap nimbly down from the back window but our cat Twinkle. From Madam's glare and comment I doubt he would have been returned home after the ride!

And yes...my car headed for the Liquor Control Board of Ontario to bring a new batch of their containers back to our scattered belongings in the recreation room...to re-pack and re-label. Finished at last I mopped my brow and admitted that those boxes, old and new, had saved the day. I'm not for drunkenness but long live the LCBO!

## 42. JUST A SIMPLE PICNIC...A MINI STORY

Back in the Spring of 1981 that fateful day arrived when Ron slipped into the Great Unknown World of Retirement. Actually he was looking forward to the freedom. What did bother him was the prospect of one of those big boring retirement bashes. Well ahead of time he cornered his replacement Don Shipston who was also in charge of the farewell. "My job has let me meet all the Hydro guys in all the municipalities of Ontario." Ron pointed out. "Why don't I just do some tours and drop in on them to say goodbye...save them feeling they have to come to TO for a chicken circuit party. It will be June so for people here why don't we just have a simple relaxed picnic." "Sounds great", smiled Don...always agreeable, and the retiree heaved a sigh of relief.

A park outside Niagara Falls was chosen as the picnic venue. Don insisted our close relatives be invited so the top floor of the Sheraton Brock was reserved for my three siblings and their spouses as well as Ron's sister Violet and our son Will...a pretty posh picnic take-off site. Our only other instructions were that on The Day we two be downstairs at the front entrance at 10 a.m. Happily it turned out to be perfect, sunny June picnic weather. The theme was to be Scottish so the guest of honour was resplendent in his Mathieson kilt, velvet Prince Charlie jacket, lace jabot and all the trimmings. I had made a simple lady's white dress (not to compete with such sartorial splendour) on which to drape my Mathieson scarf held by Ron's gift of a large cairngorm pin. I had learned long since that nobody paid a mind to me anyway when Ron was decked out in that outfit. As we waited I just hoped we wouldn't have to sit on the grass and spoil the effect of our finery.

Very soon my astonished eyes came to rest on the gleaming vehicle that slipped to a stop in front of us...a gold Rolls Royce no less! The uniformed driver leaped out to usher us into the rear seats. As we pulled away Don in the front operated some kind of broadcasting device and began an ongoing progress account of our regal journey to the park similar to the one heralding Santa Claus and his reindeers approach at Christmas..."Leaving the Sheraton Brock...proceeding to enter the highway...heading for the park...within ten minutes drive of our destination!" As we wheeled in I gasped. A crowd of 200-plus friends were clapping and shouting from their picnic tables. A kilted Scottish band struck up their pipes and escorted us to the raised platform where chairs awaited us and son Will. Don Emceed the delightful program that followed...Scottish dancers, the pipers and the band, followed by the requisite speeches by VIPS along with presentations both serious and hilarious. I don't know how Ron in his stunned state managed to rise to the occasion with a fine thank you speech. The adrenalin had taken over.

The lineup for barbecued food and trimmings gave us time to circulate and chat with all those men and their spouses whom Ron had thought to keep safely at home. "Well," I pointed out, "You did say you wanted a picnic." "Ah, yes" agreed Ron dreamily, "It was fabulous but I was boondoggled! This Gold Rolls Royce Ceilidh was not remotely or in any way shape or form even a Scottish picnic!"

### 44. HOW HARD IS A HAT?

Whenever a knock came to the door of my little home/hospital in my Abitibi Canyon days it always gave me a momentary nervous shock. Serious accidents were rare but with a 24/7 job who knew what might happen? One day when I opened the door there stood Bill Chester, the work foreman. As always his brown fedora hat was pulled firmly down on his head. As never before though, little streams of blood were dripping down from under the brim on all sides. His expression was of a doomed man!

No pushing the panic button allowed so the calm nurse ushered the victim into the hospital room…sat him down and removed the hat. A quick search located the offending cut…just an inch or so long…on the back of his scalp. A thorough washing first…hair cut around it…and finally a small area shaved to allow for a dressing to be applied. No stitches needed. A mug of coffee and some reassuring talk brought forth the details of the event.

Hard hats were available in those days but not as yet mandatory. Obviously the foreman being in charge felt outside the need for this gadget when supervising the crew operating the crane at the plant. That day however he had decided to insist that those who were not wearing them immediately do so. His approach unfortunately coincided with a swing of the crane right at his soft fedora-covered head. The sight of all that blood convinced him and the crew that the damage was mighty. Scalp wounds put on quite a show. In the end it was the humiliation that hurt Bill Chester the most.

When I was praised for taking care of this serious industrial accident I didn't see any need for pointing out that a one band-aid wound is hardly lethal!

## 44. A WARTIME SWEET TOOTH...A MINI STORY

    Unlike the Hydro community at Ear Falls, isolated Abitibi Canyon was not spared rationing during the World War11 years. At Ear Falls we had feasted on rich baking with no lack of coupons to hinder us.
    Some people suffered more than others. My next door neighbour in the Canyon and closest buddy Dot Frampton had a sweet tooth that could never be satisfied by what she considered a cruelly meagre allowance of the sugary stuff. Sitting in her kitchen having a chat one evening her usually disciplined behavior suddenly snapped. "I don't care." she announced jumping to her feet, "I am right now going to use up every ounce of our sugar and butter ration for this month and right this minute make a pan of the stickiest, gooiest Chelsea buns you ever saw...let alone tasted." Lucky for me Dot didn't plan to have this orgy alone. Out came the brown sugar, the butter, the raisins, the nuts and other ingredients. Dot hummed happily as she tossed them together, rolled them out, slathered on the goodies, rolled them up, cut them in rounds and shoved them in the oven. Keeping an eye on the clock we filled the time playing rummy. When the bell went off and the pan of golden dripping beauties came out we literally drooled...forced into a few more hands of cards rather than burn our tongues off. With the clock nearing midnight the feast at last began and ended only when our stomachs began to protest. The two "perps" felt only slightly guilty that a mere taste was left for Dot's husband and two boys. I have a feeling they may never have forgiven her.
    I don't know about Dot who would never admit it anyway but I did suffer the next day. I'm sure a sugar hangover is the equal of that suffered from over-intake of any alcoholic beverage!!!

## 45. COLOUR DID COUNT

One of my life's more exciting moments happened in 1970 when, my face pressed close to the window next to me, our plane circled down over the deep blue ocean and coral sand beaches of Bermuda. Ron and I, as guests of my sister Marjorie and her husband Walter Blackburn, were heading for a splendid vacation treat at the Coral Beach Club. Ahead were ten days of scooting from one end of the island to the other on our mopeds, swimming those blue waters, feeling the softness of the coral sand and exploring the joys of that beautiful island.

Not being golfers we could do our own sightseeing which included trying to locate a man, George King, whose name we had been given by Ron's sister Violet. One of her classmates at Trinity College, whose home was Bermuda, had a brother now a Member of Parliament in this tiny land. It was intriguing to think of getting an insider's rather than a tourist's slant on this exotic land. We had no trouble locating "The Honorable Mr. King", a tall impressive man, and were duly invited to attend ·Parliament which by a happy coincidence was in a morning session. Forthwith off we went to the two-storey square but imposing House of Parliament. I was fascinated by the fact that there was no glass in the windows. The sitting MPs paid no attention as the occasional bird made a foray in to swoop around. Discussion centred around the wrecks that had over the centuries been sunk in local treacherous waters. Designating the rightful owners was always a major part of the parliamentary agenda and could go on for years…not least because fortunes might be involved.

Afterwards our genial host suggested lunch, restaurants being within easy walking distance. I wondered when we passed several nice ones but finally climbed some stairs to his choice. Aware of our newcomer status Mr. King explained that this was one of only a few restaurants available to blacks. In spite of his position many clubs and other areas were also forbidden territory for him. After a lifetime he still found the bans difficult to accept. We had been aware of the struggle in the States but had not known that this island of British background was not yet rid of such blatant racialism.

I don't know just when those bans were lifted but for that trip somehow this experience took away some of the sheen from our view of that gorgeous subtropical paradise.

## 46. THE DEPRESSION

What was growing up in the Great Depression like for us young people? You may note that putting together the remembered facts gives some of the early Twenty/Thirty ones what I think is excusable double exposure. Important too is that we who were born between the two Great Wars didn't miss what we never had. Normal for the times, every family managed to live with shrunken funds. Children expected to wear hand-me-downs...from oldest to youngest and mended as long as they would hang together. Mending included sox (using the wooden egg) and repairing the "holes in soles". My one exciting event was thumbing through Eaton's catalogue (the only one in print) to make the agonizing choice of the one "boughten" dress of the year. Opening the parcel when it arrived was second only to the joy of Christmas morning. I did say a fervent prayer too that it would fit.

Toys? Girls had one doll to be cherished (not a shelf full), its wardrobe lovingly stitched by patient mothers and aunts from scraps of material. A little homemade wooden bed complete with sheets and a counterpane appearing on my birthday morning one year. It was like winning a lottery. The life of that Eaton's catalogue extended into being the sole source of paper dolls and their wardrobes, kept in a shoe box and traded at our Paper Doll Meetings. Clara and I trundled our precious shoe boxes back and forth endlessly. Unlike today the models stood up straight on the pages with shoulders that would hold the tabs on each cut out dress. Boys might inherit a passed down heavy metal train set sturdy enough to continue having new owners. Rite of passage for my brothers was a bike...but that huge expenditure did not extend to girls. They had to "beg to borrow" for their rides. Girls got roller skates...and barked knees which required frequent slathers with the dreaded iodine. Of course all kinds of indoor and outdoor games were enjoyed without cost.

Money? Pennies were valuable coinage. The Penny Bank system had been set up in schools. Once a week I earned an allowance of 10 cents by dusting the banisters and going to the creamery for the butter (amazing to watch the man's deft fingers wrap the pound expertly in oiled paper). Five cents was deposited in the account at school. Clutching the other nickel I raced to the shop that sold mouthwatering hand-dipped butterscotch suckers for a penny each. At one a day that left only two days to wait for the next taste of sheer bliss! One saved dollar bought Christmas gifts for all the family members.

Food? Meals were plain but real hunger was the sauce. Plates were polished clean and my eagle eye kept on my two brothers lest my cake or cookie treats be snatched.  The special rolled rib roast appeared on Sunday (no more than a dollar's worth) and even the gristly bits went down.   Cold beef, stew, liver and fish marched through the week.  In winter, pantry shelves of canned fruit replaced the fresh supply and flabby veggies from the root cellar in the yard had to do.   Doses of cod liver oil, and tablespoons of sulphur and molasses were regularly administered for good health…ugh!  The only "boughten" treats were from the ice cream parlour…nickel cones or a brick of 3-colored Neapolitan to be sliced and savored sitting on the veranda steps of a hot summer evening.

Wheels? Anywhere in town including school was "shanks mare"…the best way to meet, chat and enjoy your friends. We didn't know what a bus was and the town had just one taxi to be reserved for a rare trip to catch the train. One great game was being pulled blindfolded and giggling around town in a wagon, then guessing where you were, taking turns. No wagon fare needed.

How the beleaguered adults felt in the "Dirty Thirties" as they struggled with minimal resources we never knew.  They saved every bit of paper and string, wore their clothes beyond repair and no doubt cut down their own consumption of food in favour of their growing young. The scars from those years never healed completely.  At the same time lessons were learned that would help in the good years ahead.

When I consider the mixed-up world that the young are coping with today, to tell the truth I'm really rather proud to be a survivor of the Depression Generation.  It gets my vote all the way.

## 47. WHAT IS IT REALLY LIKE ?

Time to relax in my easy chair, and ponder a bit...putting together some "Words of Wisdom on the Subject of Aging". They belong at the end of this screed (my dictionary says a screed is usually a "long and tiresome" piece of writing). Well...it's a pretty long and tiresome process. The point I will immediately make though, the result of my own experiences, is...No one can possibly know what its all about until they get there themselves.

"Process" is the right term. I have an article on the subject written a few years ago that is far from up-to-date. I thought then it was the ultimate truth. For one thing I am still discovering that, barring physical or mental problems that interfere (as they can at any age) it is possible to get a lot of enjoyment out of the advancing years. Here is a revised version. Others in my peer group no doubt could add to it.

It's hard to believe...was it really about 50 years ago...that I was at an age to take a very dim view of that sad time of life labeled "senior"? Shopping in my local Mall in Toronto I saw so many of those white-haired oldies settled in the chairs provided...their canes and walkers parked nearby, and their hearing aids turned up to catch any gossip. How could they look so cheerful? Some had come by way of a "handicap" bus but who knows how others got there. I felt so sad for them, reduced to such a pastime. Another experience was passing by a so-called "residence"...to my mind more like a ghetto, inhabited by just that one ailing age group, even if the building and grounds looked very attractive. Anyone walking spryly in or out was obviously an employee or maybe a visitor ...someone coming to brighten the monotony of the day for an aging relative. To me it was depriving them of the pleasures of mingling with the young and lively. At that time I knew there were organizations devoted to programs just for those who could no longer join in the fun and games out in the real world...in the "Seniors' Centre" the grannies and grampas were reduced to cards and crafts and exercises that would not tax their failing bodies. The fact that they seemed quite content didn't prevent my being depressed by it.

My attitude change was gradual...simply the result of finding out for myself...aided by contact with the contrasting generation of my granddaughters. For example, much as I loved them I became alienated from their lifestyle...loud television. computers, I-pods, DVDs and then so many more techno gadgets that I lost interest in keeping track. As for music...I refused to accept that blaring noise as such. I was even grateful to have hearing aids since I could remove them and cut out the din.  I realized that I had stopped keeping track of the names of movies and their stars. The entertainment pages in the paper whose every word I had once devoured, were now in a foreign lingo...certainly not the Queen's English.  The new television shows were just a series of rapid, noisy often violent pictures that made me dizzy.  Reruns of the likes of hilarious "I Love Lucy" were a blessed gift.  Conversation was limited since my young and I were on completely different wave lengths.   As well there was the responsibility of handling any plans or problems that might arise.   I had always been independent and the one in charge. Now if I needed help with the TV or computer or one of those hold-the-line unending solve-your-problem phone calls my granddaughter would roll her eyes and take care of it in a whipstitch.  I had always enjoyed having the girls' friends drop in for meals or even overnight.  I willingly spent a day preparing their dinner.   Then I found they were happier left to themselves for pizza or a concoction of their own.  I learned to leave them to it.   And I had always loved dancing but when they began whirling around I just looked with envy and slipped away.   Hard to admit I was glad when they left and peace descended.

        Of course the inevitable event that speeded up the process was the day my son took over my dear Toyota.  It was my own decision.   After 60 years of enjoyable driving I realized my reactions were just too slow and I lost my nerve.  The government  kindly let me keep my license (with a sticker on it in case I forgot to use it only as an ID).  This critical event brought on the dependency we all dread in a world on wheels.  I had scoffed when I heard complaints as long as I was still driving.  After all there are taxis and buses.   Now I was finding it was far from being a desirable switch.    Enter endless waiting or busy phone lines plus adapting to inconvenient schedules.   On my trips to the Mall I was shocked to realize that the busy young people passing by were seeing me exactly as I had seen those pesky "seniors:" so many years ago.  It was a case of "What goes round comes round"!

        My granddaughter and I managed to prove that, with a little effort, the conflicting generations can live happily together.  We still believe in the rules (Victorian Hangover?) that weathered the Great Depression and World War11.   The two generations since then have embraced a culture that has eliminated lots of the unnecessary Do's and Don'ts.  For example...I had prepared family Christmas dinners for 60 years and the process had taken a week of hard work including setting the table days ahead of time to the last touch of perfection.   Then recently I spent Christmas with my granddaughter Vicky and her husband Scott.   They hosted three of us (Vicky's sister Jackie, Dad Will and me) in Woodstock for three days which I had dreaded.  Arrived we found that not much had been done about the festive days ahead of time. We were welcomed by the bare Christmas tree which Jackie forthwith had a great time decorating.   The men took over watching over the bird while having a male talk fest. There was time for pleasant walks and talks. Papers and other clutter was not swept from the festive board until fifteen minutes before the meal was ready and all ten participants were on hand to sit down. I can safely say I have never had such a relaxed Yuletide meal in my whole life and I enjoyed every minute of it. (Hey guys…how about next year?)

Back to Vicky and Gramma living together. It worked out as all give and take. Vicky kept her own bed instead of the one I wanted her to have. She played the loud stuff downstairs only and the dishes got washed stat and not the next day. Untidy didn't matter in her own digs and she stayed out as late as she liked but no drinks with driving (she is not a drinker anyway as it happens). The important rules stayed put . And oh how I missed her when she left!!!

Maybe these young people we love might accept our much touted "wisdom" when gently applied…not by being bludgeoned with it. And how fortunate I am to have weathered those years happily. Life still offers so much …and I am blessed with enough health to enjoy it.

So how do I feel about being a senior now? Thank goodness places like Kingston have a Grade A Seniors Centre with upwards of 6000 members and enough programs to satisfy the desires and/or needs of anyone, physically or mentally. They have crafts, entertainment and learning programs of every stripe. Far from being depressing the place is always jumping with activity and friendliness. They are out to do whatever it takes. I have been accepted by the Access Bus even though I don't need a wheelchair. Fortunately they understand the dangers of iffy balance and slow timing that can cause a fall on a rackety city bus. It is a real blessing to get me anywhere I need to go.

And what of those "ghetto" residences? That was my next step and no need to itemize all that one could possibly need in a bright uplifting atmosphere. My son's comment when he looked around was, "Why would you want to live with all these white-haired old people?" "But" I replied, "That is just the point. To each his own and these are mine."

To end the Words of Wisdom…I have a "cautionary tale" for the young. It is something my sister-in-law (now gone) told me about looking after her difficult mother in her final years. "We were waiting for a train and I told her it would be in in about 15 minutes. In a few minutes she repeated, 'When is the train coming in, dear?' So I would say, 'In about 15 minutes, mother'…and then again the same question and the same answer." Violet was philosophical. "I figured it was just as easy a system as saying testily, 'I already told you that mother.' That way she wasn't reminded of her advancing years and faltering memory."

We all need that kind of loving understanding that helps make our losses bearable and life still happily livable.

## 48. BACKGROUND STORIES

For a background we can try bringing to life the pictures of Dad and Mother, flanking the painting of the home in Strathroy in which they lived, as they gaze benignly down on me from my wall above the computer. For sure they have not a clue as to what that funny gadget could be. No wonder since Lawrence Henry Dampier (fondly known as L.H.) was born in 1854 in England (thirteen years before Confederation!) , the son of John Ludwell Dampier, himself born in 1820, the same year as Queen Victoria. I still find those far off dates mind-boggling. John had emigrated from England to Canada in 1838 along with some of his eleven siblings and settled in London Ontario. Others had scattered to Australia, South Africa and back home, with no further records. Dad's mother Sarah Edmonds was Canadian-born and Dad was the only surviving child of the union. Sarah had been the popular house mother of a now defunct boy's school in London, Ontaario, Hellmuth College, named after a local Anglican Bishop, also known for having helped to establish churches in Cuba, and Dad was educated there. A handsome engraved tray given to her on her retirement was presented to Huron College for its archives by my brother a few years back. My grandparents had also started the Sunday School for Cronyn Memorial Church in their home basement. Dad took to banking as his father had and through the years found his way from London to Stratford and finally to Strathroy near the end of the 19$^{th}$ century. One elderly friend told me that he was very popular with the local farmers and business men as he always supported their request for loans and used his clout with Head Office. In fact his bosses were reported to have had him stay in Strathroy as being too much of a firebrand for promotion. In my memory there was never any alcohol in our house but as a younger man Dad had a reputation for parties. One story goes that one night he drove a team of horses through town scattering the populous right and left. Of a Saturday night he would garner a pile of steaks and head for Bixel's brewery where he and his pals would cook the meat by way of a shovel thrust into the furnace, to be eaten with a schooner of beer. As a sober citizen he served as mayor a few times as well as on the Board of the local hospital, curled and lawn bowled and played a good rubber of bridge. I detect a bit of a knowing smile up there.

Of mother I have more bits of her life but no personal knowledge at all. Edith Isabel English was a Strathroy native, born in 1885, the daughter of Colonel John English, an immigrant from Ireland. You have no doubt noted the 31 year difference in age between my parents. Mother was Dad's second wife, he having married a friend of his daughter Helen (by first wife Louise Burwell). This lovely girl attended Bishop Strachan School in Toronto and graduated in nursing from The Evanston Hospital (Illinois) training school in 1910. I have a copy of the letter of recommendation that the Strathroy mayor (Dad) had written, praising the applicant. Neither dreamed that they would be married three years later. Their children, Marjorie, Lawrence, Edward and Mary (me) arrived in short order. Sadly neither the fifth little girl nor our mother survived the birth in 1921. Four young orphans were left when the single father died a few years later in 1930. Such a short time in which my parents were together…producing so many lives only to leave them as children.

    The bits from mother's side reach from her father's birthplace in Ireland to plantations in Baton Rouge Louisiana and to New York city before emigration to Strathroy in Canada. Colonel John English left Ireland for America in 1863 and somehow met up with and married Isabella Ulrica Donnell of Baton Rouge, born on one of their three beautiful plantations. Fact and not myth is that her mother Belle Knox was of the same family as Martha Knox, the wife of George Washington. How we love those tasty bits! A further Donnell story echoed down the years as far as us. Belle Knox had been engaged to marry the wealthier of two Donnell brothers in New York. The night before the wedding Belle ran off with the impecunious brother William Shepherd Donnell. How romantic! Trouble was that the wealthy brother was so furious he willed his millions to the New York Public Library. That one I can verify since on one trip to the Big Apple I visited the Donnell branch of the library (across form the Museum of Modern Art) and viewed the verifying plaque in the lobby. Somehow there was a vestige of his estate left to us which we managed to pry from the government in Albany…the few hundred dollars each a small memento of that Victorian drama. The final connection with those plantations came with the Civil War when three barrels were packed with the family silver and treasures before they took off for Canada. One was buried, one given to a trusted slave and the last taken along with the immigrants. Only that barrel survived and we each have a few pieces of family history to treasure.

Grandfather Col. John English holding grandchildren Edith (mother) and Uncle Arthur. Great Uncle James looks on, circa 1890.

### 49. A Letter From My Father

"1982 Culp St.                    Niagara Falls, Canada
                                  Nov. 16th, 1925

Dearest Marjorie:-
I intended to write to you before this, but my hands have been full with one thing and another, and sister Helen sent you word upon my arrival. I had a good letter from Lawrence which was very much appreciated by all here. This morning I received a letter (2) from Edward which I will answer shortly..."

The above heading is the beginning of a four-page letter written in his elegant script by our father back in 1925. It is my only personal memento of him but was too difficult for readers to decipher and so was abandoned as useless for my book. Reading it more carefully one day I was caught up in its account of the varied events in the aging single father's annual escape from the chaos of living with his four tads at home. That meant a trip by train to Niagara Falls to spend some time with his daughter Helen from his first marriage. She and husband Harold Bucke had four offspring of their own born at almost the same time as his. Dad knew they would be kept on a tight rein during his visit.

I could picture him meticulously groomed down to waxed mustache and spats, directing the driver with his cane as he hefted Dad's leather valise into the town's only taxi. We could imagine him actually dining in that exotic railway diner that we could only gape at as the train rushed past. His letter home on arrival reported quite a whirl of events arranged for his pleasure such as bridge games where "I didn't have much luck, losing to the extent of 12 points" and an afternoon tea party "which went off very nicely". One evening they were invited to a concert in a friend's home, broadcast by radio from New York. "I have never heard a machine quite as clearly and nice as this one." he reported. "The instruments and singing were quite as good as if they had been in the drawing room with us." (Note: Maybe that is why he acquired one of these new inventions…an Atwater Kent battery radio…when he was back home) A drive was arranged to Niagara Falls New York intended to include shopping for dresses for Marjorie and |Mary "as there is a greater assortment to choose from and the prices are reasonable." (Note…cross border shopping hasn't changed in nearly a century!).

A more newsworthy item which I managed to solve in this reading involved Harold Bucke who, as an engineer, worked with Sir Adam Beck, the guru of the new Ontario Hydro plant in Niagara. Harold had been in charge of a crew raising a tug which had sunk in 40 feet of water in the canal. So far they had managed to raise it 20 feet and carry it between two scows about a mile and a half upstream. He was having to start the last of the job at midnight that day, a time for the best current, and would probably be up most of the night. They had to "shut the hydro off" during their work. This was obviously a major feat.

Referring to his young, Dad always used their full names. Amazing to read that Lawrence (age 10 years) and Edward (age 9) had both written to him. It would not occur even to teenagers these days to perform such a duty. At 6 I was still spared.

So, here is Dad's social news showing how little the basics have changed…and an engineering puzzle that would definitely have a different solution in this tech age. We'll end with the last paragraph of the letter. Note how Dad managed to squeeze in the many letters in his housekeeper's…presently also child sitter's…name and the flourish of scrolls for D A D ! Writing my version of his delightful report falls short of the original script but is much easier on the eyes!

I do remember our overpowering him with hugs…welcoming him back home.

"*My best love to you all and kindest regards to Mrs. Haythornthwaite and Daisey.*
*Write to me soon.*
*Affectionately,*
*D A D*"

## 50. ANNE AND MOTHER - MINI STORY

Seeing the newspaper picture of mother in Edwardian nurse's uniform circa 1906 I was reminded that I had no record of that or any other period in her life. I was reminded again when my niece Anne in Vancouver followed her aunt and great aunt by graduating from the Vancouver General Hospital in the late '90's. As her aunt and godmother I was planning to attend the graduation ceremony...but what would be an appropriate gift to take along?

Then came inspiration. Why not find out how to contact the hospital in Evanston and see if they still had mother's records. My sleuthing was successful and imagine my delight when the current Superintendent managed to locate those ancient treasures among their archives. The fat envelope that dropped through my mailbox contained mother's application and records of her successful training. The most precious artifact though was a copy of the letter from the Strathroy mayor praising this lovely young girl as having an impeccable reputation. These treasures meant even more to me then...and still do...than to the new graduate. Nevertheless it was the most appropriate of possible gifts to Anne.

Motto...never hesitate to throw your bread on the waters.

## 52. MOHK - MINI STORY

In the 1960's our suburban church at the west end of Bloor Street in Toronto, St. Matthew's Islington Anglican, was not a place where you would expect anything unusual to happen. You can never be sure though that events won't combine some day in an exciting way.

That was when a handsome black Ugandan Wycliffe student arrived at the church to spend his curacy. It was not long before his background as a farmer at home came to light and with that also that his country's many problems were close to his heart. Among them the lack of such a basic health food as milk loomed large. Unlike packaged food milk could not be shipped and the few dairy cows were of an inferior type. St. Matthew's had an active Outreach Committee and the idea of finding a couple of the right breed to send and start a herd caught on like wildfire. Our young Ugandan with the unpronounceable name had the responsibility of using his expertise to choose the right animals. When his Canadian education ended he planned to accompany them on the ship taking them to their new home. Raising the funds went swimmingly and the plans were fine-tuned (mixed metaphors not withstanding!).

On the designated summer Sunday the front doors of the church opened wide and the choir fully-gowned in blue robes made their way, singing "The Church's One Foundation", down to Bloor Street, the traffic blocked off by a policeman. They turned west, followed by the whole congregation joining in lustily. As I passed by I couldn't help noting the man on the veranda across the street in his jeans and undershirt standing with mouth agape at this amazing spectacle. The choir led us around the corner and to the little local park behind the church. There a truck was parked and our farmer priest in clerical robes was proudly aloft at the open back door, already in charge of his bovine friends. Apart from a Moo or two it was deemed best to keep the guests of honour away from the crowd. The Sunday School children gathered with their teachers to one side, ready with cards and gifts for their counterparts abroad. The idea of children without milk was unbelievable to them. When everyone had gathered, the rector, Reg Stackhouse, opened proceedings followed by the local MPP and then the children's spokesperson nervously read their message to go with the gifts. With no further delay (we suspected the quiet beasts might have had a calming potion) their keeper waved goodbye and disappeared into the straw as the truck pulled away to prolonged cheers and clapping.

Regular reports of the long trek to Uganda were not without revealing minor crises like nearly running out of food but the precious cargo did arrive safely and over the next few years a herd developed (aided of course by a sturdy local bull) and milk became an endless gift from St. Matthew's to the Ugandan children.

Did I forget to tell you?  MOHK stands for Milk Of Human Kindness and from the heartfelt Thank You's that kept coming  back across the Atlantic St. Matthew's MOHK was just that.

Our only peek into the family past. Grandmother Sarah Edmonds Dampier, early 1800's.

Major John Lawrence Dampier of the Queen's Own Rifles, World War II.

Major Dampier at Normandy 50 years later, grieving over lost WW11 companions.

Picture of little known Auntie Vic...mother's sister.

Mother: Edith Dampier, née English.

## A PROPER ENDING

As a rank amateur, deciding to put together an assembly of stories about life in the years long gone reminds me of the time when I used to sew my own wardrobe. That meant choosing a suitable pattern... combining it with material right for that particular job...and then following the directions blindly, hoping for success. You never had any idea until you put the result on and looked in the full length mirror whether you had a winner or not. Working with the one-page-at-a-time computer screen produces the same nail-biting uncertainty. It is impossible to picture them all combined in a book format. That is the case even though I have reached the point of scrolling through the final manuscript. There is one thing though that becomes evident. I can't just let it all come to a dead end stop. The collection has an "Intro" and now it deserves "A Proper Ending".

It is obvious that the early part of the century has held centre stage. That was intentional since I had learned already with my family Memoirs that the greatest interest was in the contrast between those early days and the present. At the time I had expected to catch the eyes of seniors like myself but was pleasantly surprised to find equal interest in younger generations. Hopefully that is still the case However that leaves several decades having no place in the enterprise. That is not to say that there isn't a store of half-stories available there. Hopefully there is now some young person who, a few decades down the road, will get the same urge I have and piece their halves with those from my time to make them whole.

I can say that I look back on those more recent years as good. So important in any life, I have been blessed with a wonderful extended family through my siblings. Too many of them are on that west coast which takes Easterners and turns them into died-in-the-wool Westerners who consider a life without the Rockies and the Pacific quite unacceptable. My flying-out days are over so I have to lure those deserters east at least for visits. My own family with just me, my son Will and grand girls Vicky and Jackie, is still my anchor. Vicky chose to fly off to Woodstock in Western Ontario with her husband Scott which complicates visits, especially in winter since that is the snowbelt...frequently too risky for driving. Will is about to live in his new house up near Centreville on his beautiful piece of country land. I can't wait to be there in Spring weather when the woods and pond make a lovely setting. Our dear challenged Jackie lives away over town and too seldom can I enjoy her lovely smile and affectionate hugs. For myself, life in the Chateau Residence provides a bright upbeat atmosphere…lots of senior company…and all the amenities my age group could ask for.

It's always easy at any stage of life to find lots to complain about but being grateful for the zillion positive things we have had and experienced makes life still very much worth living. No matter how it fares, cobbling together these "Stories of My Century" has been fun and a fascinating learning experience. So…what comes next? When I don't spend all my spare time like this I can go downstairs and take part in more of the activities provided and meet more of my fellow residents. The writing itch and new ideas may even return! I hope that you all are as blessed as I have been. FINIS!

POSTSCRIPT

"A Proper Ending" has taken an unexpected twist that turns it into more of "An improper Ending"… certainly not the one planned.. My comment on the back cover that it was too risky to wait until my 100th birthday was right on. Physical problems caught up with me and I'm so glad I reached the end of my stories before having to call it a day.

Blessings to you all. Mary M

## ABOUT THE AUTHOR

Mary Dampier was born in Strathroy Ontario, the fourth child of Lawrence Henry (L.H.) Dampier and Edith Isabel Dampier on April 10, 1919. Elementary education was in Strathroy and Collegiate in London, Ontario, followed by the 5-year Bachelor of Science in Nursing course at Western University. That included nearly three years at the Royal Victoria Hospital in Montreal. Mary was married to Ron Mathieson in 1951 in Toronto. She now resides at a Senior's Residence in Kingston,

Ontario.